NOTHING
to
HIDE

NOTHING
to
HIDE

A Dancer's Life

by

ROBERT La FOSSE

with

ANDREW MARK WENTINK

DONALD I. FINE, INC.
New York

Library of Congress Catalogue Card Number: 87-46026
ISBN: 1-55611-051-0
Manufactured in the United States of America

10 9 8 7 6 5 4 3 2 1

This book is printed on acid free paper. The paper in this book meets the
guidelines for permanence and durability of the Committee on Production
Guidelines for Book Longevity of the Council on Library Resources.

For Peter Fonseca—
He made our world more beautiful.

v

CONTENTS

ACKNOWLEDGMENTS

I'd like to thank George Coleman, associate publisher at Donald I. Fine, for asking me to "tell all"; Marsha Woody Zummo for everything she taught me; Gary Lisz, for helping to retell our stories; Lola Herman, for her guidance and for Assertania; Florence Pettan, for putting me in touch with the right people; Kenneth, for some great suggestions; Newton, my Springer Spaniel, who stood by me; and my Mom and Dad, for meeting each other in the first place.

Special thanks to: Steven Caras, Reed Jenkins, Paul Kolnik, Sue Martin, Mira, Martha Swope, Max Waldman Estate, and Monroe Warshaw for capturing important moments from my onstage career in the photographs they've allowed me to use in *Nothing to Hide*.

Upon being asked to write this book, I felt it would be too big a task to accept on my own. I immediately thought of the one and only person that I had known ever since I came to New York, Andrew Mark Wentink, who has instilled the confidence, knowledge and help that I needed to survive these months, when, at times, I didn't think I would survive them. Thank you, Andy.

PREFACE

Human beings are born with the instinct to express themselves through movement. Even before he could communicate with words, primitive man was dancing to the beat of his own heart.

If you think about it, there are almost as many forms of dance as dialects within any given language. The wonderful thing about all those dance forms is that, more often than not, you don't have to know how to execute them in order to understand what they mean.

Dance is an art form. It preceded speech. We take it for granted now because we talk so much, but people used to relate through movement instead of words. But as Charles Shultz's wonderful character Snoopy once said, "To those of us with true understanding, dancing is the only pure art form." I think that's why I related to dance. It's so basic. I think human beings are all born dancers. We choose whether we want to move or not. I think the saddest thing in life is to see someone who no longer has that choice.

I've used my body ever since I was born. I use my body to express myself all the time. I was never one who expressed myself verbally. In getting back at someone who made fun of me, I would never respond in words; my body conveyed my disdain by letting their remarks pass right through me. In

1

writing this book, I've realized that there's a part of me, the art of verbalization, that hasn't really been exercised. It's something you have to study, like dance. You have to work at it. I think that's why I might be a little dyslexic. I've exercised one part of my human structure more than the other. I haven't been able to study the English language as much as I've studied the vocabulary of ballet.

I chose to become a dancer because it was the most natural thing for me to do. Learning the English language was much more difficult for me than learning to dance. I still feel that I have trouble saying exactly what I mean. Through dancing, I can be a poet without words. Of course, my dancing is for other people, not me. I can never see what I do—or "say"— the way a poet can. I can only *feel* what I am trying to express through my dancing. Unlike a painter, who can stand back from his canvas and scrutinize what he has created, I will never experience the other side of my own form of communication. I can only imagine what it must feel like to step away from what you have painted and view it with a "third eye." Although film and videotape enable us to watch what we have done, we don't really *see* it. The immediacy of the moment of movement is gone. It's simply not the same.

Why do people use their hands when they speak? Is it because words aren't enough, or does body movement enhance the meaning of what we are trying to say? Isn't it nearly impossible to say *anything* without some physical emphasis to accompany it? In many cases, actions do indeed speak louder than words.

When I was a child in Beaumont, Texas, I remember my father always saying, "Children should be seen and not heard." I think I must have interpreted what he said as "You should *dance* rather than speak." And until now, when I was asked to write a book about my life in dance, I've done just that.

—*Robert La Fosse*

Part I

LOOKING BACK

Chapter 1

MY life really began at the age of nine, when I first performed on stage. I made my stage debut in the role of a Lizard in Marsha Woody's production of *Snow White and the Seven Dwarfs* in Beaumont, Texas. Dressing up like a lizard and acting like one is something everyone should do at least once in a lifetime. Even dressed as a lizard, I felt the freedom of escaping to another world on the stage. Or, maybe I was a lizard in another life?

Anyway, I tend to remember everything from that point on, while memories of my earlier childhood are very vague. Before that, I didn't consciously think about things. With performing, I began to form an identity. I became carefree, curious and eager to learn. A large part of my personality as a child stemmed from an overwhelming desire to please my elders, for whom I had great respect. I felt only they could teach me how to become someone special.

But this is how it all began.

Not too very long ago, in a small town in Texas, there was a handsome young man named Harold Wilford La Fosse. He was an athlete and cheerleader with a sex drive that if let run wild, would go into maximum overdrive. One day in high school, Harold met a sexy young girl, Ida Pearl Jessen. He asked her to go out and she responded with a polite "Okaiy."

"But," she added, "I cain't go out with you this week, 'cause I have to go to beauty school."

"Good," Harold quipped, "'Cause you need it!"

They dated and fell in love. After school, they were married and by the time she was eighteen, she became pregnant. Their first child was a big baby boy. Naturally, they named him Harold Wilford, after his dad. He was their pride and joy.

But Harold and Ida wanted a girl. Their second child came. Still no girl. Edmund Wayne was his name. Ida told Harold that if the next child were a boy, his name would start with *R*, making the three boys' initials spell *HER*. She thought it might bring them luck for a girl when they tried again. But before they could spell *HER*, they got what they wanted. A baby girl arrived, beautiful as a saint. They named her Theresa Lynn. Actually, she was born at St. Theresa's Hospital, which might have had something to do with it. Anyway, Harold and Ida obviously loved children, because they went on to have two more.

It was four years and a miscarriage after Theresa Lynn's birth before Robert Wade was ready and/or willing to make his entrance onto the world's stage. Maybe Dad's sperm count hadn't been right over those past few years, or as Shirley MacLaine might suggest, I hadn't quite decided which parents I wanted this time around. But I came into the world on December 9, 1959, just in time for a drive home in a '57 Chevrolet station wagon and to hear Jimmy Driftwood's "The Battle of New Orleans" on the radio.

Seven years later, after a second miscarriage, Ida Pearl gave birth to Lana Louise. Where did *that* name come from, one might ask? By this time, new babies had become a La Fosse tradition, and *all* the kids wanted to have a say in this baby's name game, especially me. I insisted on Lana, a tribute to the great Hollywood star, Lana Turner. Harold and Ida wanted Louise. There was a compromise—resulting in Lana Louise La

Fosse—which, in retrospect, seems to me like one of the greatest striptease names ever.

Like most people, I don't recall being breast-fed, walking for the first time or learning to talk. But, I do remember my first day of kindergarten. The school was only ten houses down the block from my house, but at the time it was a very long walk. As I grew older, the walk became shorter.

Going to school was a big deal to me at first, because it meant I was old enough to leave home without the aid of my parents. Growing up was something I thought about a lot throughout childhood. Each year when my birthday came, I was excited to add another number to my age because I always wanted to be older than I was.

In the beginning, I enjoyed school. Learning fascinated me. It was the idea of growing up and being "an adult" that helped me to learn things then. If I were very good in school, I thought, I would grow much faster and become independent. My overriding desire was to please adults—my parents, my teachers, my dancing teacher. I worked very hard at school to bring home straight A's, but I didn't really care about what the A's represented. I just wanted my parents to think I was their smartest child. To me, "A" meant *"Approval."*

It was a rude awakening when I realized that no matter how fast I learned, I still had to go through all twelve grades. But if school was something I had to do in order to grow up, then I'd just have to grin and bear it.

Although he wasn't the eldest, Edmund was, to me, my "big brother." He was the one I looked up to, the one I wanted to be just like. We looked alike—blond hair, blue eyes, fair skin and a resemblance to our mother—but the resemblance stopped there. I was always showing off and talking back to my parents. Edmund wasn't. There's nothing worse than an opinionated child—I should know, I was one.

"Children should be seen and not heard," Dad would say to

us, again and again. I thought he meant it *literally,* which made me madder than hell! I thought it was a stupid remark. All I could see in my mind were these little children playing in a field with tape over their mouths.

Lana Louise became my "little sister," the one I thought I could boss around. Little did I know! Her cast-iron will never allowed *anyone* to persuade her to do anything against her will. She was a stubborn little tot, with a mind of her own, like our dad. Like Theresa, Lana was a knockout, but she had the most unusual birthmark on her head, which made her hair grow black in the middle of her platinum blonde locks. Lana Louise hated this sign of distinction and liked to comb her blonde hair in a way that covered it. I told her a million times that women spend hundreds of dollars to have highlight effects like that done to their hair, but Lana wanted to be like everybody else.

I was so concerned with wanting *not* to be like everyone else that I was very proud of my distinctive birthmark, a big mole on the back of my neck. I was very upset when, for fear it might be cancerous, it had to be removed.

My father worked for Gulf States Utilities in Beaumont. But his real passion was sports. Nights he would referee football, basketball or baseball in area high schools and colleges. His goal in life was to someday be professional and work in the major leagues. For a long time he tried to interest me in sports, and when I tried, I wasn't half bad. In fact, I was in Little League for two weeks, but gave it up when it got in the way of my ballet lessons.

My mother had to work because my father's salary wasn't enough to support five children. For as long as I could remember, she worked for the San Jacinto Savings and Loan. To help keep up with the housework, we had a cleaning woman Isabel—Bel for short. She had the biggest tits on the face of this earth—Dolly Parton has poached eggs compared to Bel. As if that weren't enough, I used to watch in amazement as she cleaned the entire house while smoking a whole cigarette without flicking the ash once. I loved her. I'll never forget one day when I was about ten. Trying to get a box down from a shelf in the garage which was too high for me to reach, I accidently knocked over a can and gasoline poured into my eyes. I panicked and ran, screaming, to Bel.

"Bel, will I be blind, Bel? Am I going to die?"

She laughed as she flushed my eyes out with water. "No Honey, you're not gonna be blind. Everything's gonna be just fine." Hugging me like a mother, she buried my head deep into her huge breasts.

As a child, I was rather disappointed in my parents. I wanted them to take more of an active role in my life. I wanted them to say, "You should take piano lessons and we'll pay for them." But they didn't have the money for lessons, let alone a piano. I wanted them to make me read, which I didn't do enough as a child. I wanted them to push me, but they never did.

I always wondered if my parents were as "intelligent" as parents should be. So, I searched outside the home for role models, mostly among my teachers at school. But not until I met Marsha Woody, my dancing teacher, did I find someone who I thought could show me the way. She was a very bright woman and, when sharing insights into dance with her students, impressed me as being rather philosophical.

My parents were definitely not big on philosophy or looking at "the big picture." Dinner was when most of the talking was done and it was not about "issues." When the family sat down to dinner, it was at a huge bar in the kitchen with as many stools to sit on as there were children. We never had a "formal" dinner in all the seventeen years I lived there. Our conversation concerned just about everything under the sun, but never touched on anything very deep or what to me seemed "intelligent." Our talks were always very simple, concerning practical things that had immediate effects, like toilet paper.

I remember a great family confrontation about whether the toilet paper should unfold from the bottom, or unfold from the top. Half of us agreed that you saved more on toilet paper if you unfolded from the top because it didn't fall out. My mother and my father usually disagreed and the children took sides. Since our family seemed to have an innate need to argue, I loved getting in on these conversations. It was our way of expressing ourselves. The art of formal conversation, yin and yang, was simply not there. It was just *toss* everything into the middle of the table and whoever talked loudest and longest came out the winner.

I always found dinner with my friend Kenneth's family fascinating. First of all, his family sat down at a *real* dinner table, with chairs. Their table manners were impeccable and the conversation amazingly civil. They talked about business, science and, "What did *you* do at school today, Kenneth?" It was a totally opposite experience from eating at home.

But, looking back, I thank God, for my family's down-to-earth attitude that kept us from splitting apart. Although they may not have done it consciously, the most important thing my parents gave us was allowing us the freedom to experience whatever we chose to do, without preaching about right and wrong or influencing our decisions. They certainly made their opinions known, but they trusted us enough to make our own choices. As an adult, I realized that what they gave me was much more valuable than specifics. They permitted me to find my own fulfillment, never getting in the way of my interests, especially my dancing. Most boys who go into ballet are not that fortunate, especially with their fathers.

We were sort of a popular family around Beaumont.

In junior high and high school, Harold was a three-letter man and star athlete. I grew up without him around the house very much. I was five when Harold was in his last year of high school, preparing for college and marriage. That's how I knew Harold. He had a very difficult time in leaving home, going out on his own and deciding what he would do with his life. He wasn't sure if there was life after football. I assume there was some conflict between the Harolds, junior and senior, concerning my father's desire that his eldest son become involved in athletics. Ironically, the son who eventually did what my father was interested in had more troubles than the sons who went on to careers and lifestyles he never would have dreamed of in a million years.

Edmund, on the other hand, was always involved in extracurricular activities like choir and musical comedies, and was very popular. He was outgoing and interested in people, but didn't go out of his way to make people like him. He had a tendency not to be outspoken about his personal feelings or opinions and preferred keeping his thoughts and feelings to himself.

I was like my sister Theresa, always outgoing, voicing my opinions and trying to get involved with a certain sort of crowd in order to make myself popular. It was never a secret that I wanted to be liked by everyone. I made a point of getting along with everybody but usually steered clear of people I thought were harmful. I went out for Student Council president in junior high, and ran against a friend of mine, Jan Greenspan, a sort of Charlie Brown look-alike. He was very well liked and a sure bet for the job. I wanted to be president as a proof that I was liked and was "in" with the popular kids. I didn't actually want to *do* this job.

The theme of my campaign was "Peanuts." I made these huge posters of Charlie Brown cartoon blowups, with Lucy saying things like, "Did you hear? If you vote for Robert La Fosse, he'll put Coca Cola in the water fountains!" or, "Vote for Robert, and instead of cafeteria food, he'll serve pizza!"

I was out of my mind. I didn't want to be Student Council president. I wanted to be popular. Thank God I didn't get

11

elected. I'm sure I wouldn't have even shown up at any meetings! But I had such a great time making those posters. They were beautiful. There is still that part of me that says I should have won on the artistic merit of my ad campaign alone!

Edmund left home a year after Harold. When he graduated from high school he was offered a contract with the National Ballet of Washington, where he danced for three years. That left Theresa, Lana and me at home. One year later, Theresa married Johnny Zummo and moved to Dallas. And then there were two. Lana and I finally got our own bedrooms.

I'm not sure which parent I was closer to. I had certain characteristics of each. I looked like my mother, but I had the temperament of my father. I fought more with my father because he was the one who usually could hold up his side of an argument as long or longer than I could mine. We often got into heated discussions, but they never got out of hand. While I looked to my parents for advice and guidance as a child, I knew even then that when I grew up to be an adult, I would have to deal with them as people and decide whether I liked them or not. Since we'd no longer be living under the same roof, the rules would be different.

Meanwhile, back at the ranch (house), my grandmother, Sydalis La Fosse, sat in the back room of our house, crocheting and watching wrestling matches on TV. She was Cajun French and loved to talk to my father in this dialect that sounded to me as a child like they were speaking French with food in their mouths, "Chomp, chomp, chomp, chomp, chomp." It sounded horrible. I hate to admit it, but I didn't like her very much. Always alone, she was depressed most of the time. Had I known then that her husband, Sivigner La Fosse, had killed himself, I might have understood and been more sympathetic.

Feeling she had nothing really to live for, my grandmother rarely got up out of her easy chair. A sliding door to her room was her own private entrance in the back of the house, though she never went out. A priest came every Sunday to give her Communion in her room. The idea of home-delivery Masses seemed very eccentric to me. Our family, on the other hand, went to church *religiously*, every Sunday, for fear my grandmother would make us feel guilty that not going to church was a very un-Catholic thing to do. The kids all attended catechism classes, and as children, Harold, Edmund and Theresa even went to St. Anne's parochial grade school. Lana and I went only to public school.

I never quite understood why as children we had to attend church. At the age of five or six, when I first started going to church, I barely had a knowledge of the English language, let alone the ability to understand the spiritual and ecclesiastical concepts of life, death, sin, marriage, good and evil. I just wanted to go out and swing on swings and roll in the dirt. Anything spiritual was too far away for my little mind to grasp.

None of my brothers or sisters liked church either. We were always trying to get out of going somehow. But there was always our grandmother to remind us that, after all, attending mass was one of the basic tenets of the Roman Catholic Church. I thought adults, being older, wiser, and more experienced, knew something I didn't and supposed it was all some sort of training that would someday explain itself. So, out of respect for our elders, we rarely missed those sixty minutes of total and incomprehensible boredom.

Mass was a total mystery to me. I didn't understand a thing about it. "A reading from the Gospel according to Saint . . . ," was my cue to drift off into my fantasy world. The church itself was a beautiful place and I thought the stained-glass windows were the best thing about it—five years old, and already into aesthetics! Now, if they had had dancing in church, I might have devoted more time to religion! But, they didn't. If I had known about gospel churches then, I probably would have gone. Oh, and the singing, too. I really enjoyed

13

singing and like everyone else loved to hear the choir and the organ music.

I looked forward to my first Holy Communion. Getting to stick one of those little white wafers in my mouth was the highlight. I couldn't wait till I was old enough to do that! But when the time came, I had to learn this long "speech," "Bless me, Father, for I have sinned . . . ," and tell the priest all my sins in Confession. I thought and thought, but I couldn't come up with one. In my mind, I had never sinned. I thought a *sin* was something truly bad, like stealing, or killing someone. So, when I went into the confessional, I was scared half to death. I didn't know the speech and wanting to do everything just right, I felt like a failure. As it turned out, the priest coached me through it. When I got around to confessing, I told him things that were natural for kids—I had said bad words, I had lied to my parents, and—oh, yes—I had played "doctor" with Becky in the attic. I walked out of the confessional with a mental picture of my soul being a clean slate. Having survived the ordeal, I never went back to Confession again.

When time for Confirmation rolled around, I thought the church was really getting somewhere. At Confirmation you got to choose another name for yourself. It's *your* name, why not choose it?

I always wanted to be called Christopher. This was my chance. Christopher Wade La Fosse. Or Christopher Wade. Or Christopher La Fosse or Robert Christopher or Christopher Roberts. I was always thinking of my stage name and practiced signing my name over and over. After all, I had to be prepared for all those autograph hounds when I got famous! It was something of a shock to learn that there was already someone famous with a name very close to my own—Bob Fosse.

In catechism classes we first learned the Commandments. "Honor thy father and thy mother" was easy enough. But sometimes my father spanked me and I hated him for it. I supposed it was a sin to harbor feelings of "hate" for my father, but nobody's perfect. We were also taught to "Love thy neighbor." This was a hard one. I didn't know many of my neighbors, but I figured that as I grew up, I would eventually get to know and love them all. Of course the Golden Rule—"Do unto others," etc.—seemed like just good common sense to me, even as a child. I didn't think you had to go to church to learn *that* as a rule to live by.

Then there was—"Number 7"—about stealing. I'm afraid breaking that one was too much for me to resist. Like so many children, I had the curiosity of a cat and always wondered if stealing were something I could get away with.

One day, when I was in my early teens, I went shopping at Treasure City. I had fifteen dollars in my pocket, money I had earned mowing the lawn, but I didn't want to spend any of it on tights I needed for dancing school. Once in the store I found the tights I wanted and took them into the dressing room to try them on. They fit perfectly. All of a sudden, I felt the most uncontrollable urge to commit—"Number 7"—what I thought would be the crime of the century—or at least the crime of record in Beaumont, Texas. I slipped on my jeans over the tights and headed for the door.

I wasn't five feet outside, feeling everything was under control, when I heard a man's voice call out to me, "Stop raht there, son. Where do you think yer goin' with those pantyhose?" My first impulse was to run for the Louisiana state line, or better yet, the Gulf of Mexico, but my blood went cold. I froze in my tracks. Then I thought I could squirm out of this stupid mess by handing the guy the money to pay for the tights and walk away innocent of any crime. But that was too easy. The man escorted me back into the store, where I had to give my name, address, etc., to the manager who then phoned the police.

"Oh, please, don't do that," I begged. "I promise, I'll never steal anything again as long as I live." My pleas fell on deaf

15

ears. This guy was hell-bent on putting an end to crime in the world, starting with me—"The Terror of Treasure City." Adding insult to injury, this Beaumont Javert called my parents. "Oh, God! Don't bring *them* into it," I cried to myself, "I'm already up shit creek without a paddle!"

They booked me. Or at least took my fingerprints and made a file. They didn't want my photograph. I felt almost insulted. I would've posed, gladly.

It was bad enough that my parents had to come pick me up at the police station, but I had a hell of a time explaining why I wanted "pantyhose." It crossed my mind to say I was buying them as a present for my mother, making myself look like a thoughtful son. But I could tell from the look on their faces that they'd never fall for it. They were *not* a happy couple. Looking at them, you'd think I'd robbed the San Jacinto Savings and Loan.

On the way home, I explained to Mom and Dad that they were tights for ballet, and I just couldn't resist the temptation of trying to get something for nothing. They came back with the "A-thing-like-this-could-lead-to-bigger-crimes-if-you-had-gotten-away-with-it" speech. When we got home, I was sent to my room for the rest of the evening. I was grounded. Big deal, I thought. I like my room anyway. Two hours went by and I decided to try to make a deal with my parents. I was always a pretty good actor when it came to getting what I wanted. The final decision was that I had to mow the lawn without any allowance for two months. I got off pretty easy. Nevertheless, knowing I had a police record made me feel like a juvenile delinquent for a while. The fulfillment of my ambition to be my parents' favorite son seemed to be diminishing.

But all wounds heal. My shame faded with time and my parents' love for me didn't appear to be affected by the incident, but I never tried stealing again. When I turned eighteen, the file was discarded and with it vanished the only trace of my fleeting life of crime.

Meanwhile, I went through years of Masses, with my mind fading in and out, dreaming of all the places I wanted to go and imagining all the things I wanted to be. There were times when I at least *tried* listening to the priest, attempting to understand what the Mass was all about. But I'd inevitably wind up concentrating on his bald head, watching his glasses slide slowly down his nose or wondering how much better the altar boys would look if they were all the same height.

When grandmother La Fosse died, I was in my mid-teens. Her death didn't upset me very much. I was more concerned about the fact that I couldn't cry about it.

After she died, the family never went back to church. No one said anything about this major change in family routine for a long time. Once, on a visit back home from New York, I finally asked, "Doesn't anybody around here go to church anymore?"

"No, we do other things with our Sundays now," someone in the family said. Which at the time sounded like "We got rid of the old girl, so we don't have to go anymore." It wasn't that we hated my grandmother. We respected her as our father's mother. But she was very removed from our lives—we never did anything or went anywhere with her, she never ate with us and I can't remember even getting into a car with her.

We didn't see much of the rest of my father's side of the family. They were all in Louisiana. But I was always fascinated by our French name and what it meant. La Fosse means "the ditch" or "the moat." Robert means "grand." So, call me "the grand ditch"—that's Ditch!

I was much closer to my mother's side of the family and loved her parents, Imola and Otto George Jessen. They had a nice house on a lot of acreage, where my grandfather kept a vegetable garden. There was a small garden house with plants and garden tools. We used to pick figs from their fig trees and my grandmother made fig preserves.

17

They were so dear. My grandfather was such a cheery old man. He was German and clearly loved children. I think I got my love for children from him. He always played games with us and told jokes.

"We're havin' company next week, Robby, and I don't think we'll have enough food. What do you think we should do?" Papan would tease, a familiar gleam in his eye.

"I don't know," I'd shrug, no matter how many times I'd heard the answer before.

"Well, we'll just have to put what food we've got into the mixer and make it go around!" he'd chuckle, and so did we. There was another one about the sugar bowl. I can't remember how it went, but I sure thought it was funny at the time! It was a family ritual to visit them every Sunday night. We'd make Dr. Pepper ice-cream floats and sit down and watch TV.

Maman and Papan, as we called them, had a "likin'" for roosters. There were roosters everywhere—rooster cookie jars, rooster cannisters, roosters on the cabinets, roosters on the tablecloth, everything but live roosters out in the yard.

The roosters weren't alone. There was a small room that should have been the dining room, but wasn't. Its walls were lined with bookshelves, but instead of books, the shelves held an enormous collection of salt and pepper shakers from all over the world. It fascinated me. They were made of everything from glass to plastic. Many were beautiful and there were some tacky ones, too. My favorite was a naked lady with removable breasts, one salt, the other pepper. The only thing I ever wanted from Maman and Papan was that collection and I asked if I could have it when they died. It's now mine.

One of the saddest things in my life was when my Maman and Papan had to be put in a nursing home. I suppose they were cared for all right, but I hated the atmosphere. No matter how much they tried to make it feel like home, it still smelled like a hospital. Because I thought it was just cruel to confine them, I refused to go most of the time. Even knowing they had gotten to the point where they just couldn't take care of themselves didn't convince me that there wasn't something else we could do for them.

"You've got to visit Maman, Robby," pleaded my mother. "She's going to die soon and you've got to pay your respects."

"What's the point?" I said. "She doesn't even know who I am. She's just a body now. She's already gone." I went anyway to please my mother, and I'll never forget that last visit. When we walked into the room, Maman was in bed. I don't think she even knew we were there. The sheets weren't pulled down over her feet, and I could see her toenails were so long that they had started to curl around. They were dirty and had grown thick, very thick. They hadn't even clipped her toenails. I looked at those toenails, and I looked at her and I couldn't speak.

Finally, I found my voice again as we left. "Don't you *ever* do that to me *again!*" I hissed at my mother. "It was *horrifying!*" It was very hard for me to understand then what was to be gained by seeing another person in that condition.

Many years later, near the end of his short life, my dear friend Peter Fonseca didn't know who I was either. Maybe he did, but he couldn't speak. He was all but gone. His dark eyes were expressive and opened wide but I couldn't tell if he recognized me. I would sit there, holding his hand in mine, and watch TV. I wanted him to know I was there for him. For those few minutes, it didn't matter if Peter knew who I was or not. What mattered was that he didn't feel isolated, that he wasn't being left to die alone. That's when I understood what my mother was trying to say about my grandmother.

Chapter 2

MY brother Edmund was a hero to me. I looked up to him almost as a second father. He always did what he wanted to do. He won lots of medals for roller-skating, which, in Beaumont, Texas, was not a very masculine thing to do. If you weren't on a football, basketball or baseball team, you were not considered very much of a man. Boys who studied music, acting, dance, were fairies, sissies, wimps. Edmund knew that his rollerskating wouldn't take him very far and soon found himself with the chance to accept a scholarship to the Marsha Woody Academy of Dance. Our father had second thoughts about Edmund taking dancing lessons, but he always allowed us to do just about anything we pleased—especially if it didn't cost him a cent.

Edmund started with tap and jazz, and acrobatics, then added ballet. He was a natural dancer—co-ordinated, physically supple, musical—and a good height at that. Marsha Woody was an excellent teacher; a disciplinarian with a very strong will. She presented the best dance recitals in Beaumont every other year at the Beaumont Auditorium. She made Edmund work very hard in class, but he also had to work for his scholarship by vacuuming the carpets in the studio lobby every night after class.

I remember going along with my mom and dad to see

21

Edmund in class on Parents' Day. That's when the curtains were drawn from the big glass wall and the parents saw how their children had progressed. That's where I met Marsha Woody.

On one of those Parents' Days, I was with my family and Marsha came up to us. "So, Robby," she said, smiling, "when are you going to start coming to class?"

For the first time in my young life, I was speechless. All this ballet stuff was kind of silly to me, but tap and acrobatics looked like a challenge that I was willing to take. She then turned to my mother and said, "I think it's time to get him started, if he's interested." I was five years old.

My first class was acrobatics. My body was as unruly as a newborn colt's. At home in the backyard, I practiced cartwheels, somersaults and splits. I mastered the first two, but couldn't quite get all the way down in a split. Girls always seemed to have an easier time at it. I had made it as far as the spring recital—"Peek around your partner, stand up big. Peek around your partner, stand up big. Runny, runny, runny, all the way around. . . ." (See, I still remember!)—when Marsha told my mother that my young body wasn't able to keep up with what I wanted to do. She thought I ought to wait a few more years and, if I still was willing, come back.

Little did they know that I was already in love with the idea of being old enough to start dancing for real. Nearly four years passed before I took my next dancing lesson.

With the exception of Harold, every child in our family took ballet at one point or another.

Theresa was too short and plump to be a ballet dancer, but she was very strong-willed and had lots of what she always called "common sense." Realizing her dancing skills were limited, she concentrated on school life. Theresa may not have made the best grades but her good looks and even better instincts got her ahead. She fell in love in junior high and married the same guy after they graduated from high school.

She was prom queen and he was quarterback of the football team, the ideal teen-age romance.

Being the last child, Lana never had a tough time. I think of all the children, she had the best physique to be a dancer, but she lacked the desire. She excelled in gymnastics and went on to be a cheerleader in junior high.

I was nine years old when I started back to dancing lessons at the Marsha Woody Academy of Dance. It was a Wednesday afternoon and the class was acrobatics. All I had to wear were some crazy black and white plaid pants, not the usual black. The following Monday, I had my first tap and jazz lesson. Same pants. I really wanted black pants, but my mom refused to buy any for me until she was sure that this was going to last more than a week. It did.

I remember my first ballet classes very well. Marsha told my mother I would now need tights and a dance belt. The tights were readily available, but the dance belt had to be special ordered. So, I wore my underpants under the tights for those first few classes. Putting on tights for the first time wasn't at all an unnatural experience for me. It felt very much like something I had done many times before. My first encounter with a dance belt was a different story.

I stood in the dressing room at Marsha's studio, staring at this thing—a sort of glorified cross between an athletic sup-porter and a G-string, worn by male dancers to "keep every-thing in place" and protected—and couldn't figure out which way to put it on. Did the wide part of the fabric go in front and narrow part in back, or vice versa? Obviously I was too young for my anatomy to dictate the answer. So, I opted for the wide part in back. Made sense to me, my butt was bigger than my front! For my next class, I tried it the other way just for kicks, and it felt much better. I've worn it that way, the right way, ever since!

When I walked into that first ballet class, the room was full of little girls, some older than I, some younger, all bigger. I was scared to death. Not of ballet, but of the effect it would have on my life if and when the kids at school found out. I wondered if I'd be able to face them. But I mustered up courage and wasn't going to let that stop me. Something felt very right about these classes, even though I knew this was not what a "normal" boy was supposed to do. I began to realize I was now "different"; yet I still wanted to be *liked* by everyone. Just because I loved to dance, was that reason for anyone to dislike me?

Compared to my ballet training, phys ed in school was a joke. To this day, I'm not sure what the school thought physical education meant. Taking the name literally, I thought the classes were supposed to educate us about our bodies through an exercise program, weight lifting, aerobics, and, god forbid, maybe even dancing. But in my school the roll would be called, a whistle blown and we'd play whatever sport happened to be in season—football, basketball, volleyball, track, baseball. I certainly had nothing against those sports, but it was obvious that many of the kids were out of shape and their bodies were not being "educated." Granted it could be fun, but I took using my body seriously, and preferred to dance. By the time I reached high school, dancing lessons took up so much of my time, I asked my mother to write a letter to the State Board of Education saying, "This boy spends every night of his life dancing for four hours, and there's no need for him to participate in this PE program, when it's not giving him half as much of what he gets in dancing." They took me out of PE. In high school I got involved in a program stipulating that if you had a job from one to five, you only had to take the compulsory courses. I immediately went out and got myself a job in the mail room of the White House, a department store in downtown Beaumont.

My mother also wrote to the state to get my driver's license early, because I had no way of getting to dance classes before my parents got home from work. She was a very clever woman in getting things done for her kids.

When dancing entered my life, I finally had something to think about during school when I got bored with my studies—which was often. I didn't really mind school as long as I didn't get bored. I never missed many days at school because there was a perfect-attendance award at the end of the year. I wanted that so badly, but something would always happen and I'd have to miss one or two days. Yet, knowing I was near perfect was fine with me. I brought home A's and B's instead. In my mind, I was my parents' best and most loved child because I made the best grades.

I've had a lifelong problem accepting criticism. I always got very defensive when I'd get corrected or if there was a difference of opinion. Except with Marsha Woody. It seemed she had all the right answers and always made perfect sense.

I "adopted" Marsha Woody as my "second mother." After all, it got to the point where I spent more time with her than with my own parents. I wanted to live with her. She had wonderful taste in clothes, furniture, manners and food. She was financially well-off. Her husband, Mike Zummo, was part owner with his brothers in a meat company, Zummo Meats. Ironically, Theresa's husband was Johnny Zummo, one of Mike Zummo's nephews. So, in some weird Texas way, I *was* related to Marsha Woody Zummo.

There I was, literally following in my brother Edmund's footsteps. I never looked at it that way, but the fact that other people did would later have an effect on our relationship.

Anyway, this singing and dancing stuff was fun, but I knew the time would come when I'd have to grow up and make a living at some sort of profession, like a fireman, a lawyer, a doctor or a policeman. I had absolutely no idea that you could get paid for doing ballet and musical comedy. I thought those people had regular jobs during the day like my mom and dad. How could anything that was so much fun be a job?

So, I didn't take dancing that seriously. In fact, I didn't take anything that seriously. I was having too much fun. I just wanted to show off, to be the center of attention, and to be in a musical show—like Edmund. I had seen him perform in a high-school variety show, singing and dancing to "Thank Heaven for Little Girls" from *Gigi,* and had to restrain myself from running up there to join him.

When I was eleven, I read in the newspaper that the Beaumont Community Players were doing a production of *Gypsy* and they needed young kids to play newspaper boys. I went to the store and got the music and lyrics to one of my favorite songs at that time—"Georgy Girl"—and the record, too. I'd sing along with that record a hundred times a day until I nearly drove my sister Theresa crazy. She finally got so sick of hearing it she told me to knock it off. "You can't sing, anyway," she snapped, knowing what would get to me. I ran to my room, riddled with insecurity, and sank into a depression.

Despite Theresa's assessment of my talents, I made it to the *Gypsy* audition. I only had to sing "Georgy Girl" and dance around. The piano started. I was a bundle of nerves. Despite the hundreds of repetitions at home, I clung to the sheet music for fear I would forget the words. But when it came time to dance, being on stage seemed quite a bit different. I wasn't nervous anymore. The power I felt while I danced assured me that I had gotten the part. Of course the fact that only four boys auditioned for four parts must have had something to do with it! But I felt lucky anyway. I was going to be in a musical comedy!

Oddly enough, I never really concerned myself with Edmund's being ahead of me. There was never really any conflict. Edmund was always very helpful to me. I think he started feeling more secure when I started taking ballet. (There were always other boys in the school, but few—Glenn Edgerton of the Joffrey Ballet being a major exception—would

26

ever become professional.) He was proud of me and happy not to be alone anymore. Nevertheless, we weren't especially close. I never put myself on his level as a child, because I was still very young when he went off to be a professional.

But from the outset, I looked to Edmund as my "mentor." He worked hard all the time and sweated more than anyone I've ever seen in any sport or sauna! (To this day, whenever he pirouettes, this shower of water sprays from his curly blond locks like a water sprinkler.) He was the only example I had of how male dancing should look; my guide to learning how a male dancer dances and handles his partner. Marsha could explain, but in a feminine way. She openly admitted there was only a certain level to which she could teach and then it was time to "let the birds go and fly to new heights." Recognizing her own limitations was one of Marsha's remarkable traits as a teacher.

As I started taking my dancing lessons more seriously, there was a lot in school that I knew I would never use. I told myself I already knew what I was going to do with my life after high school, so cheating became a way of getting through school for me. I'd always cheat. It became a skill in itself. I mastered the best forms of cheating. When the teacher had her head down, I wouldn't just bug my eyes out and stretch my neck. I'd get right up from chair, walk over, look at someone's paper, then go back and sit down. It was outrageous. I really knew how to cheat. I'd wear long sleeves and have notes all over my arm. I'd have papers shoved in my socks. All the classics.

Cheating was a means to get through an experience that, at the time, I had difficulty in accepting. Had I known how much I lost by not learning things on my own, I probably wouldn't have done it. I spend a lot of my free time now catching up with the general education I cast aside then.

When Edmund graduated from high school he was offered and accepted a contract with the National Ballet of Washington, where he danced for three years. When I first saw him dance with the National Ballet, a real professional company, in Lake Charles, Louisiana, I realized how good he was in relation to other ballet students. I finally understood then where I fit in. Before that, I had been told that I was talented, but I couldn't tell.

When you're a ballet student out West somewhere, you have questions about the real level of talent in New York. Having no standard for comparison, you don't know where to place yourself in regard to what you've been given and what your true talent is. In dance, you can rarely rely on your own instincts or the image you see in the mirror, to evaluate your own talent. You're always on the inside looking out, never on the outside looking back, so to speak. You never really know.

When I was fourteen, one of my great desires was to live in New York and finish high school by correspondence. I knew it would never happen, so I contented myself with going to New York for summer dance programs. It wasn't until I finally got the chance, with my parents' permission, to earn my own way to New York for the first time that I discovered for myself where I was and what I was really going to do with my life.

When I first started dancing, I wasn't crazy about ballet. I loved tap and jazz, performing in local musical comedy productions. My love for theatre became clear through these experiences. I knew it was where I belonged. But, *whatever* I was going to do with my life, no matter where I ended up, no matter what I was going to be, I was going to do it in a grand way.

Chapter 3

WHEN I was twelve or thirteen, Marsha Woody formed the Beaumont Civic Ballet and presented a full-length production of *The Nutcracker.* I was Fritz; a Mouse; and in the Russian Trepak. In the spring of 1974, I heard from Jimmy Emerson, a friend in the company, about auditions for the upcoming Orange Community Players production of *Oliver!,* in July. I had seen the movie and had always wanted to do the title role. Having performed in Marsha's recitals, in school plays and *Gypsy,* I didn't find the idea of auditioning the least bit frightening. I wanted to be well prepared, however. I bought the soundtrack album and spent weeks studying every nuance of the role for the audition.

At the audition, I recognized a boy I had seen perform an amazing skit in elementary school. He was first to audition for the role of Oliver. He had the Cockney accent down pat, he could sing and was a natural mover. The boy's name was Kenneth. Seeing him, I felt my chances were in jeopardy. Scott Sigler, a boy from Orange, was next to audition. His reading and dancing left a lot to be desired, but he sang even better than the boy in the movie. Eventually my turn came. I knew I had certain things over both of them. I looked like the movie Oliver, and I could dance better.

Kenneth and I were the final choices, but the director

couldn't decide which of us would play Oliver and which the Artful Dodger, the other lead. He had us read the same scene over and over, switching roles. We both wanted Oliver, but whatever the final decision, we knew we would be playing opposite each other in the leads. I felt Kenneth had the upper hand because being such a good actor, he could do both roles equally well. I hadn't seen myself as the Dodger and was definitely weaker in that role.

In the end, Kenneth, despite being younger and smaller, was cast as the Artful Dodger, the older role, and I was Oliver. Kenneth and I immediately became best friends. We had everything in common. It didn't take long to find out that even though he was about two years my junior, Kenneth seemed several years my senior in intellect.

Orange was about thirty minutes away from Beaumont, and we had to commute. One of the guys working on the show was from Beaumont, and we often hitched a ride with him. His name was Art. He was twenty-five years old, extremely handsome with long brown hair and very easygoing. By profession, he was a physiotherapist who worked with learning-disabled and slow children. He had a van and smoked marijuana. I liked him a lot.

One evening in the middle of the rehearsal period for *Oliver!* it got too late to drive back to Beaumont after rehearsal. As he usually did when that happened, the director asked Kenneth, Art and me to spend the night at his place. We were put up in the living room, Kenneth and I in trundle beds, Art on the floor. Kenneth immediately drifted off to sleep. I was very tired and wanted to go to sleep, but couldn't with my brain filled with the excitement of the evening's rehearsal. Something else was exciting me, but I didn't know what it was. I lay there tossing and turning, looking out the window. I noticed that Art seemed to be having trouble getting to sleep, too, but thought nothing of it.

Suddenly I felt a hand on my foot and heard Art's voice

whisper, "Robby, would you like me to massage your feet? It might make you fall asleep." My feet *were* sore and tired from rehearsing, and a massage might be just what I needed, I thought. I didn't know, I had never had one. I agreed, so Art asked me to get down on the floor in order not to disturb Kenneth.

The reflief of tension I felt with the pressure of his hands on my feet went straight to my head, enabling me to relax as I never had before. He then started rubbing my calves and thighs. As he worked up my back, easing the tension, he eventually positioned himself on top of me. Our skin touched and I liked what I felt, but wasn't sure why. I was embarrassed to feel turned on by all this. We didn't say anything. We didn't have to.

My God, I thought, this is the greatest feeling I've ever had in my life. I can't say that what was happening upset me. In fact, it seemed to be the most natural thing in the world. After all, two people touching and caressing has been around for quite a long time. By the time Art got up to my neck, I was fantasizing about feeling the pressure of his full weight. As if reading my mind, he leaned forward, started to massage my head and lay on top of me. I felt like the world was spinning and didn't care if it ever slowed down.

Nothing happened that I could be ashamed of, but I wondered what the sensation of kissing him would be like. There was something between us. I wasn't sure *what* it was, until the night he invited me to his house for dinner. He lived out near Lamar University in an old, run-down Victorian house with interior decor that was real "sixties"—tapestries, incense and Phoebe Snow singing in the background.

We started cooking spaghetti and meatballs and Art asked me all sorts of interesting questions about myself—a subject I always enjoyed talking about. Then, while I was stirring the meat sauce, he came up very close and put his arms around me and gave me the tenderest of tender hugs.

31

The feeling of Art holding me like that frightened me at first, but when my heart started beating again, I let my feelings take over. Art never had to ask me if I minded his doing this. It was obvious that I had no problem entering into this relationship. It didn't matter that many people considered it wrong for two men to feel this way about each other. I only knew that I felt comfortable with this quiet, gentle man and thought this could have been a relationship with a woman, but it wasn't. I now had a secret I felt I could never tell anyone, especially my parents, Marsha Woody—or even a priest.

After we ate the spaghetti, Art and I sat talking about his life and work, the different girlfriends he'd had, the work he was involved in at the moment, the hiking and camping trips he'd taken. I imagined us somewhere in the middle of the woods, alone forever.

Well, being the "stars" of *Oliver!*, Kenneth and I became spoiled brats. Knowing they couldn't find anybody from Orange to do the leads made us feel like the most important thing since Wonder Bread. Since there's not usually a big budget for most community productions, you usually take care of your own costumes. Kenneth and I, of course, had to have the most terrific costumes. We went out and shopped for fabric with an eye out to making our costumes look as close to the movie version as possible. Movies were the *rule*. Movies were what guided your whole perception of how things were done.

As a precaution, the director decided on having understudies from Orange for me and Kenneth, just in case we couldn't make it in from Beaumont at the last minute. We kept telling him not to worry about it, but a lot of good that did! As time went on, he felt that since the understudies had rehearsed as much as we had, they should be given a chance to perform it at least once or twice. And we *hated* it!

My understudy turned out to be Scott Sigler, the one with

the beautiful voice. Even with rehearsals he still couldn't act his way out of a paper bag. It was phenomenal. He could sing, but when he had to speak, his Cockney accent sounded like he was from, well, where he *was,* which was southeastern Texas. Despite what Kenneth and I felt about our understudies, they got to do one performance. The rest of the time they were orphan boys in the chorus.

The day before the understudies' performance in the leads, Kenneth and I got to talking. "You know what?" Kenneth said, "What do they think they're going to do for a costume when they do the leads?"

"Well, I suppose they figured it out," I said, wondering what he was driving at.

"No, I don't think they have. I think they assume they're going to be wearing *our* costumes," he said.

"Oh, *really*?!" I said, raising an eyebrow. There's a certain tension, a competitiveness among kids that can be very devilish. Adults are expected to deal with situations on a more upfront level. Kids think they can be openly outrageous and get away with it.

Without a word to anyone, Kenneth and I made plans. The next day, when we were to replace our understudies in the chorus, we left our costumes at home in Beaumont! Performance time rolled around and the local leads were without costumes. Fortunately, Scott, as Oliver, could use his orphan costume from the chorus, but he had nothing to wear when he had to get dressed up later in Act II, when Oliver is taken in by the Bronlows', his upper-class patrons. But as the Artful Dodger, Kenneth's understudy, Jim Vosseller, needed a major costume, which couldn't be just whipped up. In true theatrical tradition, the Orange Community Players managed to throw something together at the last minute.

We caught *hell.* They wouldn't let us live it down. Everyone went on about it and called us "divas." But we felt so satisfied! We didn't need revenge, but there was some sort of great

33

pleasure in doing what we did. It was our way of saying that we didn't need understudies . . .

But we didn't stop there. Since Kenneth and I were the only people in the show who could really dance, the choreography was sort of freestyle in the "Food, Glorious Food" scene. So we were determined to stand out by throwing in somersaults and flip-flops, just a few tricks here and there, even though we were warned not to do anything our understudies couldn't do. "Are they kidding?" I fussed. "Do they want us to be boring, just because our understudies are?"

Kenneth and I became best friends by being thrown together by Fate. Although our houses were very close—his backyard ran into the schoolyard of our elementary school—we really didn't know each other. I had first seen him in one of our little talent shows in grade school. I was in the fifth grade and had done some acrobatic number I had choreographed to "Spinning Wheel." Kenneth was in third grade. He came out with a cardboard fruit stand and did a whole Charlie Chaplin routine with a banana. He was a cop and Charlie Chaplin at the same time. He kept running in and out from behind the set, slipping n the banana peel, and changing costumes . . . It was the most insane and sick thing I had ever seen in my life! I loved it! It was the best thing in the whole talent show, needless to say. It had production, acting . . . everything. He was just one of these born-funny creatures. I never forgot that performance, but we never got together until *Oliver!*

After *Oliver!* Kenneth signed up for classes with Marsha Woody and got a scholarship. He became my little "protégé" and started to look up to me. Kenneth was small for his age and his natural ability for ballet was not as great as Edmund's or mine, but he was strong-willed and smarter than most dancers. He was excellent in tap. He played the piano. I was jealous that not only did his parents let him *play* the piano, they even *had* a piano.

In junior high, Kenneth and I were in choir class together, which was composed of different grade levels since it was based on singing ability. We both had very high voices and sang louder than anyone else. But the choir teacher, Walter LaForge, always gave us the lower parts that we didn't want. Kenneth and I were always getting into trouble. We sang the wrong notes on purpose, we threw paper airplanes and we talked a lot. It seemed we spent at least half our chorus time on the way to the principal's office.

At first, Kenneth was involved in theatre more than dance. There were regular seasonal performances out at Lamar University and Kenneth made his L.U. debut playing a child in the play *Ice Bound*. He did lots of musicals: *Annie Get Your Gun*, *The King and I*, *South Pacific*, *Guys and Dolls*, but other than *Oliver!*, none that I was in.

In 1979, two years after I left Beaumont, Kenneth planned to move to New York to pursue a career in musical theatre. His timing was perfect. I had just rented my first studio apartment at Broadway and Sixty-ninth Street, and I invited him to share it with me. Kenneth arrived in New York the same day I moved in.

"Don't you think we should have a loft built over the closet?" I asked, looking around the empty room.

"Sure," he answered matter-of-factly, "only it should be over the kitchen." Within minutes, Kenneth was on the phone ordering the lumber. Within forty-eight hours, we had it installed. I immediately saw the benefits in having such an efficient roommate, who also happened to be your hometown best friend.

The first few years I lived in New York, I was very into "what was hot and what was not." I used to go to record stores and ask the clerk what the top seven or eight best-selling albums were, and then buy them all. They were usually bad, bad disco. One of these times, shortly after Kenneth arrived, I came home with an armful of records and told Kenneth that the man in the record store said these were the hottest records in New York.

We put one on the turntable and played the first cut. It was awful. We tried the second. It was worse. The third. The fourth. We tried the flip side. They were all interchangeably bland and horrible.

"Robby," Kenneth said, "this sounds like the shit my sister would listen to."

"You're right," I said. Without another word, I took the record off the turntable, we marched to the window, Kenneth opened it and I tossed the disc scornfully into the middle of traffic on Broadway. Five months later, the album won six Grammy Awards. So much for the taste of the disco generation!

Chapter 4

I didn't start taking dance until I was nine and in the fourth grade. Up until that time, everything was fine as a child. The "problem," such as it was, began when I started going to junior high.

First of all, I was interested in choir, which is almost in the same league as dancing. Being interested in music and choir at school sort of puts you in the same category as the "rah-rahs," they used to call them, the "goody-goodies." This was one of the many categories that kids in school naturally fell into whether they wanted to or not. You had your jocks on the sports teams, and there were bookworms, who never seemed to be very attractive, but they made great grades. I'd always become friendly with those people so I could cheat off of them! I stuck with them, because they were very valuable to me for getting ahead in school with the least amount of effort.

When it got around that I was taking ballet, there were kids who called me names, the usual "ballet boy" or "sissy." The ironic thing was that, in a bizarre sense, I was popular because of it. It wasn't the kind of popularity that most children of that age want to have. Most children want to be student-council presidents, or cheerleaders, or athletes or whatever.

It's interesting what makes children popular. Being a good athlete is usually a guarantee. There's the group that come from wealthy families, which makes *them* popular because they seem so confident and get cars before everyone else. Then there are popular personality traits, kids that are just funny, the "class clowns," everybody likes them. And there are those whose good looks make them popular.

There was a couple in fifth grade who were the first ones to start "going together," you heard about them being "in love" with each other. When we started going to junior high, they would always be in the back of the bus, kissing. They were "cool" because they were in love.

.Even as a kid, I always tried to be "fashionable." Dingo boots, which had squared-off toes and big clunky heels were popular at the time. Naturally I had to have a pair. I saw in a magazine somewhere that it was trendy to stick blue jeans inside your Dingoes. Girls had done that, but no boy dared try it. One day, I decided to be a trend-setter. It lasted half a day because everyone stared and made fun of me behind my back. I tried to grin and bear it, but finally decided it really wasn't worthwhile. I just couldn't deal with the humiliation of it all and gave up on trying to make a fashion statement. So I took my jeans out of my boots and that satisfied everybody.

Girls would always say, "Oh, you're so great! You're taking ballet. You know what you're going to do and you're going to have a career and become famous!" I was always very popular with the girls, and they wound up being my friends. I felt comfortable with them because they accepted me for what I was. So I had the girls on my side.

Boys seemed to be a little scared of me, because they weren't quite sure if they wanted to be associated with a "sissy" or someone who took *ballet*. I was sort of slight and I guess a little flamboyant, qualities one would associate with a ballet dancer. I didn't look or act like your typical hefty football player or the out-of-shape guy in the band. When I was very small I often went with my family to Kelly High School basketball games to watch their star, my brother Harold, play. One of those times, the cheerleaders got hold of me. They thought I was "so *pretty*," they wanted to put lipstick and makeup on my face. They loved the result, which made me look like a little girl. My mother thought the girls were "just havin' their fun," and I didn't think a thing of it.

But then, I had few "hangups," and don't feel I have too many now. I don't recall ever coming home from school saying, "Oh, I can't go to school because of what they're saying . . ." School was sometimes a struggle, but I learned to enjoy it. I gradually discovered that being different from everybody else, perhaps even a little controversial, was more interesting than being liked by people.

Nevertheless, the comments about my being "pretty" or taking ballet weren't always easy to take. There were two guys in junior high who cornered me and actually wanted to beat me up because I took ballet. Even then I wondered, Who *raised* these kids?! The comments were usually ridiculous, inane ones because those kids were putting down something they knew nothing about. They had no idea of what it was like to go and actually take a ballet lesson. They were putting down something in the same way that I might put down football. I had nothing against football, I just didn't like it. Whenever someone ridiculed me, I was usually speechless. These people were small-minded, I thought, and would never get anywhere. So as I went through school, I worked up a determination to prove that I was going to make something of ballet and show them all. For the ten-year reunion I grandly planned to show up in a limousine and throw copies of *Time* magazine in their faces. I knew that in ten years many of them would have gone to college and still wouldn't know what they were going to do with their lives. They'd have babies and divorces and finally realize that I wasn't fucking around.

Those years of dealing with peer pressure and ridicule

helped develop a certain strength of character, a certain "backbone" in overcoming people's objections to my individuality, that I'm grateful for. Even at the time I did my best to overlook it by thinking, After all, at three-thirty I'm out of school and into my own world in ballet class. I felt that as far as life itself was concerned, I was actually about twenty steps ahead of most kids. I knew what I wanted to do with my life. Most of them were going through high school as if it were Life itself. Which was fine, I guess, becuse they were having a good time. But I had a dream that couldn't be realized in Beaumont. I couldn't wait to be someplace where people didn't think you were a "sissy" if you took ballet; where I could dance as much and as long as I wanted with others who loved dancing as much as I did; a place where I could study with great teachers, and learn by watching the greatest dancers in the world. I longed for New York City.

The young couple, Harold and Ida Pearl LaFosse.

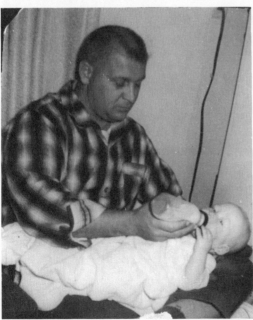

Harold, Sr., with Robert Wade
LaFosse, 3 months old,
(March, 1960)

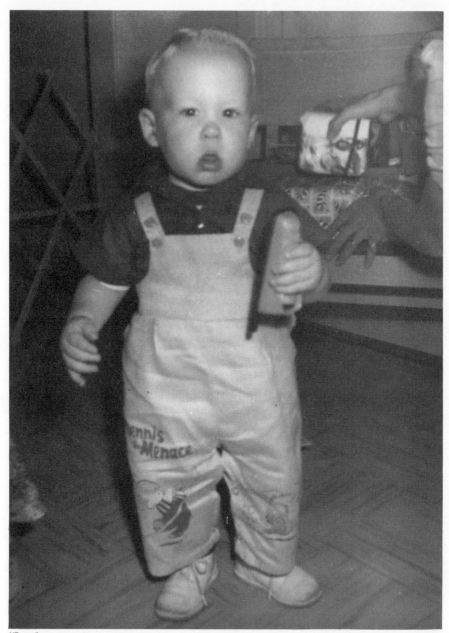

"Look at me, I'm walking!" Age 1, (December 1960)

"All in the family"—almost (Lana Louise hasn't arrived). back row, l to r:
Harold Wilford, Jr., Edmund Wayne. front row, l to r: Robert Wade, Harold,
Sr., Ida Pearl, Theresa Lynn, (1965)

My First Holy
Communion—with tie
(like my "halo"?) slightly
skew! (May, 1967)

Ready for the Easter Parade with my "little sister" Lana Louise (Easter, 1969)

Brother/Sister Act—"partnering" Lana Louise (1973)

With Kerri Blake, my date
for the 8th Grade Prom.
(I chose the outfit!) (1974)

Performing in a grade school talent show—no one looks too impressed!

Marsha Woody, my first dance teacher
in Beaumont, Texas. (1969)
". . . the best dancin' teacher I ever
had or will."

With fellow Marsha Woody student,
Glenn Edgerton, now with the Joffrey
Ballet (1969)

As "Fritz" with Kelly Hafley as "Clara," rehearsing for the first Beaumont Civic Ballet production of *The Nutcracker* (1971)

As "Oliver," with Kenneth Ammenhauser as "the Artful Dodger," in Orange Community Players production of *Oliver!* (July, 1974)

As "Peter," with "Hunt Ladies"
(l to r: Shannon Gillett, Debra
Broussard, Jaylene Hamm) in
Marsha Woody's production of
Peter and the Wolf. (1977)

A "disco period" portrait in my
Patricia Fields jumpsuit. (1978)

Part II

AMERICAN
BALLET THEATRE

THE SCHOOL OF AMERICAN BALLET, INC.

LINCOLN E. KIRSTEIN, PRESIDENT
GEORGE BALANCHINE, CHAIRMAN OF FACULTY
NATALIE MOLOSTWOFF, EXECUTIVE DIRECTOR
NATHALIE GLEBOFF, ASSOCIATE DIRECTOR

April 22, 1977

Mr. Robert LaFosse
5280 Cambridge Lane
Beaumont, Texas 77707

Dear Mr. LaFosse:

We are pleased to confirm your acceptance into the five week Summer Course at the School of American Ballet.

I understand that you are applying for a scholarship and so I am enclosing financial aid application papers. Will you have your parents fill out the form and return it along with a Xerox copy of their 1976 Income Tax Return?

It will be submitted to the Scholarship Committee who will give you a prompt decision.

We look forward to having you at the school this summer.

Sincerely yours,

(Mrs.) Mari A. Cornell
Secretary

Chapter 5

I moved to New York in the summer of 1977. The previous two summers, I had received a scholarship to study with the respected teacher David Howard at the Harkness House for Ballet Arts on East 75th Street. The first year, 1975, I didn't have the money for airfare to New York, expenses or a place to stay once I got there. My parents said they couldn't do a thing about it. I knew then that if I was going to get there I had to do it on my own. I got my first job at thirteen, bussing tables in a restaurant. I was too young, but they hired me anyway—my brother Harold knew the owner. In one year, I earned enough money for a summer in New York. Although very hard work for an adolescent, it was an experience that taught me how to earn and save my own money, giving me a sense of independence at an early age. In the end, I was glad I wasn't one of those children who rely on their parents' financial support for everything, taking it for granted.

During those summers, I stayed with Edmund, who by then was a leading dancer with the Eliot Feld Ballet. In 1975, he had an apartment on West Seventy-third Street. I realized for the first time that summer that I was really serious about this "ballet stuff."

After the six-week 1977 summer session at the School of American Ballet, I had a moment of fear of ever finding a job.

But as fate would have it, I was walking down Broadway and ran into Rebecca Wright, then a leading soloist with American Ballet Theatre (ABT). I knew Becky from class at Harkness House and admired her as a performer. She asked me if I was going to continue my studies at the School of American Ballet (SAB) through the winter. I told her I wanted to stay another year at SAB, because I didn't feel ready for a professional company, but I couldn't afford to. I would have loved to study one more year before getting a job.

Becky told me that Miguel Sanchez, a corps de ballet dancer in ABT, was leaving the company and they were looking for a replacement. She told me to call Florence Pettan, secretary to company director Lucia Chase. What did I have to lose? At the very least, it would be good experience. And I loved ABT.

In early 1975, I had seen a performance in Houston, Texas a two-hour drive from Beaumont, that confirmed my love of ABT. It was *Coppélia,* with Mikhail Baryshnikov and Gelsey Kirkland. I gasped along with everyone else at Misha's astounding leaps and marveled at Gelsey's adorable character and perfect technique. I could understand why they were the biggest sensation to hit the dance world since Fonteyn and Nureyev with the Royal Ballet in the sixties. They were perfectly cast as those characters. To this day, I think it was the best role I ever saw them dance together. The kids from Marsha Woody's school and some from Houston had gathered in the lobby to critique Act I. One girl said she heard that Gelsey Kirkland was a real bitch in rehearsal. I answered that it didn't really matter what she was like in real life. All that mattered was what she did onstage. And on stage she was breathtaking. That performance awakened my desire not only to dance with, but to be a "star" at American Ballet Theatre. How could I turn down a chance for a job there?

I called Florence, and an audition for me to take company class was set up for the following week, on a Thursday. I showed up at the audition feeling completely out of place.

With the exception of a few dancers like Peter Fonseca and Cheryl Yeager, who I knew from David Howard's class, the other faces were new to me. I was in awe of everyone—really "stagestruck." But I was also shocked—they all were much shorter in person than they appeared on stage!

I stood at the barre in first position, ready to give the performance of a lifetime. My eyes scanned the room in search of Lucia, but she was nowhere in sight. Jurgen Schneider, a ballet-master imported from Germany by Baryshnikov, taught a class that was very "Russian"—a style unfamiliar to me— and I had a very hard time. Still a rather weak dancer, I couldn't keep up very well technically. I managed to cover up by "performing."

After the barre work, we came to the center. At that moment, Lucia Chase arrived, escorted by ballet master Scott Douglas, a former ABT principal dancer. Her red hair wispily coiffed and wearing a conservative green dress, Lucia smiled amiably as she walked with a distinctive shuffle to her chair. It was hard to believe that this rather diminutive, unassuming woman was one of the most powerful figures in the history of American dance. Throughout the rest of the class, she and Scott would eye certain dancers then, after each combination, whisper to each other like prospective buyers at a horse auction. I remember pirouetting exceptionally well in that class. Sometimes nerves and adrenalin can give you ability you didn't know you had.

The company dancers were getting back into shape after a long layoff. Most of them were sore from the barre exercises and didn't stay for the end of the class. So, only a few boys and I stayed on for the last big jump combination. Here a dancer is expected to execute difficult steps like double tour en l'air (jump up, turn around twice in the air and land softly)—a challenge akin to hitting a "high C" or a home run. The combination was longer than I was accustomed to, and I had trouble remembering all the steps. At one point, I went in the opposite direction, almost crashing into soloist Charles Maple, but I executed it with such conviction that everyone else must have thought *they* were wrong!

Despite everything, the audition went well, but I knew I wasn't strong enough yet for a major professional company. It was then that I really began to worry about how I was going to support myself during another year at the School of American Ballet. Would I have to wait on tables? As I was leaving the building, Scott Douglas caught up with me and said, in his raspy Southern accent, "Stick around. Lucia wants you to come back tomorrow. She's not quite sure yet if she wants to offer you a job."

I was still rather short, only 5'6" or 5'7", and very skinny. I was seventeen, but looked thirteen. I just wasn't ready. I'm sure Lucia must have been desperate, because if someone older, or taller, and more experienced had been there, I'm sure she would have hired him over me. After the second audition, I got the job. Lucia offered me a six-week apprentice contract with the condition that if she liked my progress, I would be offered a full corps de ballet contract.

The very next day, I was thrown into a rehearsal room to learn "The Waltz of the Flowers" in Baryshnikov's *The Nutcracker*. My partner was a beautiful corps de ballet dancer named Cynthia Harvey, whom I also knew from class at Harkness House. Cynthia was very helpful and considerate, making it much easier for me to learn the steps. I couldn't believe how fast Jurgen Schneider taught and expected a dancer to learn the choreography. So, I was surprised when Jurgen called upon Cynthia and "the new boy" to demonstrate the proper way to waltz. In Texas, I had always had months to prepare. Now there were only a few weeks to learn the repertoire before ABT's fall season at the Metropolitan Opera House.

I wasn't the only new boy in the company that season. They had just hired a boy from the School of American Ballet, named Patrick Bissell. He was very tall, with the all-American build of a football player. He had masculine charm and a big talent to match his stature. His future with ABT seemed promising, especially since his height made him an ideal partner for tall ballerinas like Cynthia Gregory and Martine van Hamel.

After years of watching from the audience, I suddenly found myself in rehearsals with Mikhail Baryshnikov, Cynthia Gregory, Gelsey Kirkland, Ivan Nagy, Natalia Nakarova, Fernando Bujones, and other great stars. On the surface, I tried not to let anyone notice how impressed I was, but inside I was still a fan, a kid with his dream of stardom.

While at the School of American Ballet the summer I got into ABT, I took some extra classes from David Howard at the Harkness House. After class one day, I spotted a pair of Gelsey Kirkland's pointe shoe shanks—the hard insole that strengthens the shoes, but which ballerinas often take out in order to flex the shoes into being more pliable—and took them. I didn't know what I would do with them; I just wanted to have something of hers. She was, at that point, one of the most celebrated ballerinas in the country. Perhaps it was simply the challenge of managing to get them at all that interested me.

Later that week, I asked Gelsey to autograph them for me. "How can you be sure they're mine?" she said, pouting. My bubble burst. I couldn't come up with any better reason than that they were her size, from her special shoemaker, and that I saw her take them out of her shoes, but I said nothing. She signed them as if it were a chore, a burden, a hardship for her, and turned away. I stood there amazed, but it would take a lot more than that to take the stars out of my eyes—Gelsey was still my favorite ballerina.

I found during those first few weeks that I was able to learn steps very quickly—a good way to advance rapidly in a ballet company. A dancer never knows when he might be called upon to replace someone in a ballet at a moment's notice. And that's exactly what happened. For a while, I thought I should have changed my name to Miguel Sanchez, being that I learned every one of his parts. Sanchez had been in a lot of ballets corps, so I had my work cut out for me. I learned at least eight ballets in my first season with ABT.

My first professional performance in New York was on September 20, 1977, at the Metropolitan Opera House—the "Big Time"! I didn't know about the "Old Met," and thought that all the greats from Pavlova on down had once graced this stage. Later I found out I was wrong, but I saw a model of the original Metropolitan and wished it still existed. To hear artists who had performed there talk about it with such feeling made me realize that a grand old piece of our history had been lost. Oh, America! Land of progress! What a shame.

My first performance at the Met was in *The Nutcracker*. I was a soldier in Act I, and in the corps de ballet of "The Waltz of the Flowers" in Act II. The most exciting part of the performance wasn't being on stage—I had been on stage so many times before—even if it was "The Met." Besides, they weren't very big parts. It was being *backstage* that was absolutely incredible. The sets and props for the Metropolitan Opera Company were all around the massive backstage area, and you could wander through bits and pieces of magnificent historical periods and exotic corners of the world from the tombs of Egypt to the bohemian cafés of 19th century Paris. They were like parts of oversized, dreamlike jigsaw puzzles challenging you to piece them together into a whole, and it was a heady experience.

The mere size of the Metropolitan Opera House itself is mind-boggling. There are two rehearsal studios downstairs, one large, one small. The stage is also used for rehearsals during the day. The corps dressing rooms were on the second floor, with rows and rows of lockers and dressing tables. I found where my friend Peter Fonseca was stationed and set up camp next to him.

Peter Fonseca was unlike any friend I had ever had. Born in Costa Rica, but raised in Washington, D.C., he combined arresting dark-haired, dark-eyed Latin looks and radiant charisma with an outrageous American sense of humor and wit. Peter was genuinely helpful. He helped me adjust to the theatre, to meet other company members, and to learn new ballets. He even taught me how to apply professional stage makeup. From the start I admired Peter as a person as well as for his dancing. They were very much the same—pleasant, gentle, elegant, and most of all, *giving*.

Sporting a new beard, Misha came back from a layoff to mount his new production of *Don Quixote* for the 1978 spring season at the Met. His version was based on the Kirov production, but would have more dancing. He was a natural at setting a ballet. The steps just flowed, at least in embellishing the classics.

Gelsey was to be Kitri, and she was working on her Spanish arms. I was in the corps de ballet and Scott Schlexer and I had to do one step across the stage with her in the first act. We had tambourines, and were supposed to follow behind her shaking them, while she did little bourrée steps across the stage. It was supposed to be very hotsy-totsy. We were just corps boys shakin' our tambourines and doing our Spanish-flavored hootchy-kootchy. For some reason, Gelsey didn't like the way Scott and I "related" to her and finally asked us to come work with her acting coach. I thought it was rather odd to seek guidance for something amounting to little more than a crossover, but I thought, What the hell! Sure, I'll go. I'll do anything once.

We went to Gelsey's acting coach and spent time analyzing who we were, where we were from, how we knew Kitri. I thought it was all pretty silly. Anyone who's been on stage for any length of time can figure out some sort of characterization for himself in a role without spending hours' more time than

57

it's worth. I wondered if we really needed to be taken by the hand and taught this. In the end it didn't do any good anyway. Surely there was no recognizable difference in our performance from the audience's point of view. But Gelsey felt very uncomfortable with us and finally got two other boys to do the part. But it wasn't really even a "part." It was action, background, atmosphere. So Scott and I decided that if Gelsey was going to get all hot and bothered about it, we would be happy to sit down upstage with the rest of the kids and have a good time. So for Gelsey's performances only, Scott and I sat out the crossover, which we did with every other Kitri!

But of all the *Don Quixote* stories, there's one I'll never forget. Yoko Ichino and Danilo Radojevic were dancing Kitri and Basil, and everything went smoothly until the third act. Just as they began the famous pas de deux, Danny got a cramp in his leg, couldn't continue and had to leave the stage. There was a long pause. Thinking fast, Yoko called to Peter Fonseca, who was in the classical corps with me, "Peter! Get out here." So Peter jumped right in, finishing the pas de deux brilliantly, with Yoko smiling all the time, saying through her teeth, "Turn! Stop! Run to the other side! Lift me!" None of us on stage could believe what we were seeing. Any dancer basically knows the *Don Quixote* pas de deux, but Peter pulled it off with amazing aplomb, as if he had been cast in the role. Yoko and Peter finished the pas de deux and the fans went wild. They took their bows and came offstage.

In the meantime, ballet master Jurgen Schneider had left his seat in the audience, came backstage and went directly to Charles Maple, who was dancing one of the soloist roles with Gregory Osborne. Jurgen was interested in boosting Charlie's career and told him to get out there and do the variation. Rather tense and not very strong, Charlie got through it, but not very confidently.

During Yoko's variation, Jurgen was backstage frantically coaching Charlie for the à la seconde turns in the coda. Everyone was backstage waiting to go on for the big coda and finale and someone asked, "Well, who's going to do the turns in the coda?" "Well, of course Peter will do them," I piped up. "He turns *much* better than Charlie!" I didn't realize Charlie was standing within earshot. My intention certainly wasn't to hurt his feelings, but I was telling the truth. Peter had amazing, beautifully soft turns. So Peter Fonseca went out and finished that performance of *Don Quixote* and because of my "artistic advice," unfortunately, humiliated Charlie Maple.

I remember another *Don Quixote* during a winter season in Washington, D.C., this time with Fernando Bujones and Cynthia Gregory. Fernando was mid-air in a grand jeté, and the lights went out. It was a cliffhanger. No one knew if he landed or not!

We eventually found out there had been a citywide power failure. The audience wasn't permitted to leave, but the dancers were allowed to go back upstairs to the dressing rooms to check on their belongings. When we came back down, the emergency lights had come on. The orchestra was still in the pit and the dancers came back on stage. The curtain was raised and we all sang Christmas carols. The orchestra played waltzes and we improvised dances. Fernando did a tango with Alina Hernandez. Peter Fonseca did à la seconde turns. I was still a young corps boy, so I felt I couldn't take center stage—yet. The audience sang along and applauded. It was like a big wonderful Christmas party at Kennedy Center. We must have been there for forty-five minutes, dancing and singing, waiting for the lights to come back on. Finally, we all left, and just as we walked out of Kennedy Center into a hushed, pitch-black Washington, lights started to twinkle back on.

ABT got a lot of fan mail from that evening. The company offered to refund ticket money, but as far as I know, very few, if any, accepted the offer. I'm sure many in the audience felt that they had gotten almost double their money's worth, first to see the company in the production the way they expected and then to have the rare opportunity to see the dancers as real people. For our part, we got to relate to the audience in a much more intimate way. The magic barrier of the pro-scenium was broken and we dangled our legs and feet over the front of the stage. It was one of the easiest but most re-warding performances I've ever done!

Chapter 6

EVERY three years the dancers, along with their union, AGMA, negotiate a new contract with company management for more money, better working conditions and other concerns. In July 1979, the negotiations with ABT were especially difficult and led to a lockout of the dancers. I faced an indefinite period of unemployment without benefits and, not being paid what the principal dancers make, which was considerably more, was not looking forward to hard times.

On July 19 from out of the blue, I received a phone call from the Broadway legend Gwen Verdon. I had seen her in *Chicago* and, like everyone else, thought she was terrific. As I listened, I couldn't believe my ears. Why would Gwen Verdon be calling me, for godsakes? Thinking at first that it might be a prank, I almost hung up on her. But as she continued to speak, I slowly recognized that inimitable raspy, sexy, little-girl voice of hers.

At the time, she was in charge of Bob Fosse's hit show *Dancin'*, and she called to tell me that the lead dancer, James Dunne, had accidently cut his finger very badly and was unable to continue with the show. His role, originated by former ABT principal dancer Charles Ward, was considerably balletic. Although there was an understudy, he was not really technically equipped to handle the role every night. Gwen asked me if I'd be interested in taking over the role for six weeks, giving me one week to learn it.

I was dumbfounded. I really didn't know what to say, but I affected my best business voice and said I would have to speak with ABT and get back to her. She gave me her phone number and told me to call her back as soon as I knew. Moments after I hung up, I realized that I didn't have to ask *anybody's* permission. Since the company had no scheduled engagements until the fall, I assumed we wouldn't settle the contract and be back to ABT for at least a month or two. I was basically as free as a bird.

I sat there stunned by the best professional offer I had ever had—and I had Gwen Verdon's phone number, to boot. All at once, I let out an enormous scream and started dancing around the apartment like a maniac. All kinds of thoughts raced through my mind. I had never seen the show, but frankly, I didn't really care if it was good, or even how big the part was. When I got around to thinking about it, I had no idea who would have given my name to Gwen Verdon, or if she knew anything about my amateur musical-comedy background. Was I going to sing? Was there anyone I should call for advice?

When Kenneth got home, I was still ecstatic, jumping up and down and telling him all about the call. He just stood there looking at me.

"You're the luckiest person in the world," he said, with a wry smile. "There are thousands of kids out there taking singing, acting and dancing lessons, busting ass at auditions, and *you* get phone calls *asking* you to do a show, sight unseen." He was utterly amazed.

I called Gwen back and told her I'd love to do the show. She invited me to see *Dancin'* that night. Rehearsals would start the next day. Gwen Verdon is one of the most natural people I've ever met. People who have that "star quality" you see on the Tony Awards show aren't like that offstage. It's "show biz." When I got to know Gwen Verdon, after spending evenings at her home, as I later did, I was able to separate her from her public image with the flaming red hairdo, brief costume, and kooky sexuality. That's simply her public image, the one that made her a success with the public, a "star."

The audience loved the show, but I frankly didn't think too much of it. However, I was too excited by the thought of dancing on Broadway to let a little thing like my personal taste get in the way. The role was larger than I thought and was technically very demanding. Since I would be taking over on such short notice, I only had to learn the solos and duets. The understudy would dance the role in the group ensemble numbers. I would be in five scenes, the hardest of which was a long solo to percussion at the end of Act I. It was a nice solo, but I could see how a Broadway dancer would have trouble with the ballet technique, especially the many pirouettes and double tours en l'air.

The rehearsal week went by in a flash with the help of Bob Fosse's assistant, Christopher Chadman, who choreographed "Yankee Doodle Disco," the finale of the show. I couldn't believe how impressed the other dancers in the show seemed to be with my work. I was a little surprised myself at how easily I adapted to the "Fosse style." The only advice Fosse gave me came after a performance during my first week with the show: "Really good, Rob. Really good. Just one thing. You've *got* to change that name!"

"If it worked for you, Bob," I said, laughing, "it will work for me!"

The day of my opening, Tuesday, July 24, was nerve-wracking. I worked with Ann Reinking on "The Dream Barre," the opening scene, where I played a "nerdy," repressed ballet student, and ran through the "Percussion" solo. I got through the whole show and couldn't remember what I had just done.

But the fact that I was on *Broadway* was a dream come true—Wow! Those were the best six weeks of my life, and it went by all so fast. Although I never wanted it to end, before I knew it I was back to rehearsals at ABT in the corps de ballet by the end of August. Misha had moved to the New York City Ballet in the summer of 1978 and our box office had suffered significantly as a result. A new career on the Broadway stage seemed more and more appealing to me. It was the fall of 1979. I had been in the corps for more than two years and I was getting bored. I hadn't been given any solos to speak of and my dream of stardom wasn't materializing. Was I in the wrong field? My thoughts turned to Broadway again and again. I was convinced that Lucia Chase didn't think I was anything special. She had just hired the Australian Danilo Radojevic as soloist, and Johan Renvall, a Swedish-born dancer, for the corps. They were both short and blond, like Misha, and very talented. It seemed clear that their presence in the company would hamper my chances for advancement and shove my career further into the background. I was not about to be overlooked in the corps de ballet for the rest of my life. I'd prefer to be a checkout clerk at the A&P. I began to envy waiters for making more money and probably leading happier lives.

Now, with a Broadway show under my belt, I began to question my choice of ballet as a career. I thought again and again about quitting ABT to pursue a life in the theatre. I would study acting, take singing lessons, find an agent. It didn't take much looking. An agent had seen me in *Dancin'* and wanted to represent me. His name was Bob Duva and he represented many of the dancers in *Dancin'* and *A Chorus Line*. I signed with him and for the next year had lots of auditions for commercials and Broadway shows.

My good fortune over the next year seemed to tell me that Fate was pushing me in that direction. In August 1980, for example, Jack Hoffsiss, Tony Award–winning director of *The*

Elephant Man, asked me to appear with the New York City Opera in his production of *The Student Prince.* Jack had me cavort around as a Pan figure, who seemed to tie together the plot and keep it moving; then, at the same time, I got a "Dr. Pepper" commercial, featuring Mickey Rooney. He was wonderful to work with, and his spontaneous stand-up comedy routines during breaks were hilarious. Even though his digressions delayed attempts by the crew and director to get back to work—after all, time *is* money—I don't think anyone minded. It was four days of grueling round-the-clock work, (I literally had to race against time to get from filming on the Lower East Side to the *Student Prince* performances at the New York State Theater at Lincoln Center) but the money I earned from that commercial equaled my annual salary at ABT. Again, I thought . . . if I made only two commercials a year, I could make enough money to live on while studying for a new career—as a Broadway "star."

Chapter 7

WHEN I had my first long layoff of five or six weeks from ABT, it took me a week just to *relax*. I would wake up every morning apprehensive about what I had to do that day. My mind was ticking and my body was still going on the ballet season schedule. The second week I was finally ready to relax, but I didn't know how. I had to consciously learn *how* to relax. My body wound down, but my mind had to adjust. By the third week, I started to get bored. I think it would take at least a full year for an active dancer's body to completely relax.

When you finally go back to work, it takes the same amount of time that you were off to get back to the level you were at when you stopped, when your body could sustain five or six hours a day of rehearsal and performance. Vacations are very difficult, but you need them every now and then just to let your body do nothing but rest.

A dancer's body takes on a mind of its own after a while. Your body wakes up quicker than your brain. You can get up and go through your morning routine, and your brain isn't really there yet. You're standing in the shower, but your mind is still making coffee.

It's hard for non-dancers to understand how a dancer's body runs on its own schedule, which is only intensified by living at the hectic pace of New York. Dancers normally live on such a tight schedule that when you have two hours off, you're so revved up you can't figure out what you want to do. Read? Take a walk? The laundry? Or do you just want to take it easy?

After a performance, it takes at least another two or three hours for the body to completely relax. You've not only gone through an exhausting physical experience, your mind and your nerves have been keyed up to deal with facing thousands of people. A lot of time you're dealing with fans.

Given the thousands and thousands of fans who consider ballet such an important part of their lives, it's interesting that so very few actually ever get in personal contact with the dancers. However, there are some who do, and, to a certain extent, you can sense whether a fan is going to be harmless or troublesome. Occasionally your instincts slip.

I was in the corps de ballet at ABT on tour in L.A., when I received a letter saying,

> Dear Robert La Fosse,
> I have been going to the ballet for many years, and have enjoyed watching your progress in the company. I am thirty years old and want to start ballet. But I have a problem. I went shopping for a dance belt and couldn't find the right kind and decided to make my own. Could you please send me one of your old dance belts that I might use for a pattern?

I was in shock. At first I didn't know if I should tell anyone, but the next day I told Peter Fonseca. Peter cracked up laughing. That day he had gotten the same letter from the same person. Soon after that, David Cuevas got his, then Charlie Maple and Richard Schafer and Michael Owen and Rodney

68

Gustafson. I don't think this character stopped before he hit an even dozen. We were amused, but none of us wrote back.

I also get a letter about twice a year from some man. It's always the same, a form letter. He only wants a photograph, that's all. Each time, he says he's starting a photograph collection and wants a picture of me. He must have about five or six by now. At first I didn't think about it, then I thought he might have lost the last picture, then I thought, This guy must make a mint on selling autographed pictures of dancers!

There was one man who sent me a letter praising my performance in some role and asked me out for a drink. He told me he had met me at a sponsors' cocktail party. I went and checked up on him and heard that he was married and had a good job, etc. It sounded harmless enough to me. But when I met him for the drink, expecting to meet his wife, it turned out he was gay and had divorced his wife eight years ago. I don't think I was tricked, I just didn't get all the right information. In any case, I had a drink with him and told him about my interest in choreography, and he immediately told me that he invested in shows and films and that perhaps he would be interested in backing one of my ballets. With that, I saw through the situation and what the terms of the backing would be. But I was very cordial, had another drink, said "Thank you very much" and left.

But the majority of the fans are wonderful, and they have one trait in common—they want to do something for you beyond just applause to show their appreciation. If they want to talk or go to lunch or dinner, what's a few minutes or an hour out of my life to make someone happy?

There are very loyal ballet fans everywhere throughout the United States, but in New York they're nearly as devoted as Mets fans—which is like having a full-time job! They go to the ballet every night, getting standing-room or cheap tickets. Leaving the theatre after performances, we see them waiting at the stage door, not to get autographs, but standing there just to be close. I wonder what goes through their minds. Is it frustration? Did they at one time want to be dancers? Or is it that they're so in love with dance they form a special bond, a kind of love relationship, with the dancers?

The most dedicated fans always know everything. They're up on all the latest gossip. They hear the rumors first. The ironic thing is, they make a point of separating rumor from truth. Having lived around the dance world so long, they know which sources are the most reliable.

Then there are the famous fans—famous, that is, among the dancers. "Coffee-Shop Charlie" Wigler, after years of unfailing devotion to the New York City Ballet, eventually got himself a job at the School of American Ballet. I think that's a great accomplishment. He's happy. He loves dancers, and now he's around them all day long.

There's "Fran the Fan," who gave herself that name. She's touchingly loyal to a handful of dancers, and I'm lucky to be one of them. She brings flowers to us nearly every night, and always on debuts and first performances of the season. Her flowers are a poetic reminder that she's there that night. Fran's the only fan I know of who has managed successfully to get backstage on a semi-regular basis. Sometimes I think the guards down at the stage door think she's a relative, because she's there as often as a doting mother or sister.

Many fans look at dancers as fantasy creatures. They're almost scared of us, and because they find it so exciting, they don't want to break the fantasy (even though at the same time many of them would probably love to have a National Enquirer of the ballet world).

I know I used to feel that distance from Gelsey Kirkland, Cynthia Gregory and Fernando and Misha. I put them up on pedestals. They were my idols. I felt I would never rise to their level. There's something fantastic about that kind of awe. When you get to know these dancers, you realize that their art form shouldn't be confused with their personal life. You begin to realize that fans don't idolize the *person*, they idolize the *art*.

Our work day isn't nine to five. It's class and rehearsing from ten-thirty to four-thirty or five, a break for dinner and then back to the theatre at six-thirty or seven for makeup and warm-up, then performance from eight until ten-thirty. It's a twelve-hour-a-day, six-days-a-week job, with no long break where dancers can have peace and quiet and do what they want to do. There's hardly any time to have dinner, let alone *make* dinner, read, call friends, have a real social life. It's very complicated. When that one day a week during a performance season comes, the number of things to do is so overwhelming —shop, clean the apartment, do the laundry, see friends, pay the bills, make appointments—that I sometimes don't do *any* of it. Lots of important matters get put aside until a layoff. There's not even a consistent schedule to latch on to. It's always different. I have days where I rehearse from twelve to two with no performance, and days where I rehearse from twelve to six, and have a performance at eight and dance two ballets. Your existence becomes a little schizophrenic. Life becomes day to day, ruled by the next day's rehearsal schedule.

It's hard to deal with that kind of existence on a year-in, year-out basis. You have to work yourself up psychologically to a level where you can be spontaneous enough to accept whatever the schedule asks of you that day. That's why a lot of people think dancers are obsessed by what they do for a living. It becomes more than a job. It's not just a daily thing, it's an *all-day* thing, and even if you're not scheduled to dance, the ballets could be changed or you might have to replace someone at the last minute. You're on call until the curtain goes up and sometimes until it comes down.

Surrounded by dance for so many of their waking hours,

dancers can think or talk about little else. We are not, as a rule, obsessed by, but possessed by it—a real difference. There's no time during the day when you can say, "That's it. It's over for the day." A lot of dancers try very hard to find that time, but when you first join a company, it's very hard to find time to focus on your personal life. I tried—with a vengeance.

Every Saturday, a group of friends, sometimes my brother Edmund, and I would get together and go to Studio 54, the former television studio turned disco, the "hottest spot" in New York in the seventies. After a performance ended at ten-thirty or eleven P.M., I'd go home, grab a bite to eat, call friends and plan what outrageous getups we'd pull together for that night. We'd meet around one A.M. because things didn't really get started at Studio 54 until about two A.M.

Marc, the guy at the door, had a thing for Robin Hardy, one of the girls in our group, so we always got in immediately. People would line up at the door, sometimes waiting more than an hour in hopes of getting in. We'd arrive and Mark would make way for us through the crowd, like Moses parting the Red Sea. It was my first taste of how being a "celebrity" must feel. In fact, Studio 54 was the place where everyone could feel like a star. It was the epitome of the Warhol dogma "Everyone can be a star for fifteen minutes."

Once inside, we'd walk down this dark corridor with ornate chandeliers. It was very glitzy. In the disco itself, the former studio, blazing lights hung from the ceiling, much as they would have for a television production. Blaring disco music pierced our eardrums and Donna Summer, at the height of her success, and Grace Jones were frequent guest stars.

We danced endlessly and the sweat ran off our bodies. It was an orgiastic aerobics class. People would drink, take drugs, or both. You'd work yourself up into such a state, you'd tolerate things—like drinks thrown down your back—that you'd never let pass under normal circumstances.

Everyone was "onstage," performing, trying to outdo each other. Since some of us were dancers, we could do some very theatrical things. One of our favorite tricks was when two of us, usually myself and Brian Jameson (who danced with Edmund in the Feld Company), or sometimes Edmund, would lift our friend Patricia Miller, a Joffrey dancer who had extraordinary extension, over our heads in a split and parade around the packed dance floor, while Pat, high above the dancers, would grandly acknowledge the cheers of the crowd.

It was the disco period, the epitome of the "Me" generation, the tinsel twilight of the "Do your own thing" era. It was total freedom. Although Studio 54 was considered very "trendy" and was frequented by celebrities like Bianca Jagger, Andy Warhol, Calvin Klein, Rudolf Nureyev, Liza Minnelli and Bette Midler (who I danced with in my red long johns!), Studio 54 never had an elitist feeling. One of the reasons I liked Studio 54 so much was that it was a mixture of all types of people. There were artists and theatre people, there were business-men and waiters; there were New Yorkers, there were Texans, there were straights, gays and lesbians; there were blacks, whites, Orientals, Hispanics. There were exhibitionists, and then there were politicians (which, come to think of it, are pretty close to being the same thing!).

But, like anything that is free without restraints, there is a fine line between fun and tragedy. There's the story about one man on drugs who wanted to get into Studio 54 so badly that he tried to crawl in through an unused elevator shaft and fell to his death. At the end of the night, or more likely early the next morning, you'd be walking out and see people who had OD'd and died right there. It was frightening. As Dickens said about a much different situation, "It was the best of times, it was the worst of times."

At the best of times, Studio 54 was like a Fellini fashion show. The point was to be as "off-the-wall" as possible. It wasn't who you were or what you did, it was how you *looked.*

Giving free reign to your imagination, you'd try to outdo everyone else with outlandishly original costumes. There was one woman who always showed up as a "poodle." She was completely naked except for pasties and a tail of strung-together ping-pong balls stuck up her butt. She was always very exposed. But that was the point. Even people who came dressed in formal evening clothes sometimes would wind up taking off nearly all of their clothes.

I once wore a bright fuschia-pink jumpsuit, hood and all, from Patricia Field. I looked like a psychedelic astronaut. One Halloween I showed up as a Pierrot, complete with tulle collar, bloused shirt, clown-white makeup, beanie hat and a drawn-on tear. I designed an outfit for Edmund of a cut-up pair of black tights reassembled with safety pins, black belts and suede Musketeer boots.

One of the most unforgettable evenings I remember at Studio 54 was the night Steven Rubell, one of the owners, took a group of us to see the "basement." That was where all the VIPs went to hang out. We were told the basement was where "it was happening." At first glance, it was just like any other basement, a bunch of lockers where the busboys and waiters kept their things, a ceiling lined with exposed pipes. But then there were wicker chairs where people would go to get away from the deafening music and masses of writhing bodies. There were people in corners having sex, and people doing entire pharmacies of drugs.

I made one truly great friend at Studio 54, Gary Lisz, an extremely talented and successful Seventh Avenue clothing designer. A bright blond Puck, Gary was often taken for a dancer because of his naturally well-fit physique. He had the comic sense of a court jester and knew how to appreciate people with flair. Two of his friends, Arthur and Kevin, were drag queens who were together at Studio every night, regular fixtures, and everyone knew them. Arthur wore sequined gowns and shaved his head; Kevin, with crew cut, featured Dior. They weren't just "in drag," they were a walking production number.

One year my parents came to New York to visit Edmund and me, and we took them to Studio. Here they were, Harold and Ida Pearl, in the infamous, notorious Studio 54, Sodom and Gomorrah reincarnated. Naturally we introduced them to the drag queens. My father seemed fascinated and actually got into a discussion with one of them. I suppose he wanted to know why on earth a grown man would want to dress up as a woman. Meanwhile, I pulled my mother onto the floor to dance.

My parents seemed to have a wonderful time. We were out until three A.M., a far cry from their usual routine in Beaumont, and I thought they were adorable. They were so out of place, yet they accepted what they saw as a part of what life was like for us in New York. For the first time, they could see with their own eyes what Edmund and I had been telling them about over the phone. I was very proud of their reaction to it all. The next day, I asked my mother what she had thought of the night before. "Well, Robby—" She hesitated. "I just don't know. I had a lovely time and all, but how do you do that *every* week?"

"*Stamina*, Mother," I said. "You build stamina!"

Going to Studio 54 was actually a two-day affair. I'd get home early (and sometimes not that early, like ten A.M.) Sunday morning and crash, sleep 'til about three or four that afternoon and wake up feeling like shit. It wasn't unusual to feel incapable of ever getting it together enough to deal with the next day of work. But the next day would come and you'd feel fine, eager for next Saturday to roll around.

Like every nightclub, Studio 54 was a place of sexual confrontation, but it certainly wasn't just a pit stop for picking up boys and girls. Of course there were people, from the rich and famous to the trendsetters and star-fuckers, to the man on the street, who came looking for a night's adventure or potential prospects for a weekend at the house in the country.

Studio 54 was so chaotic and loud, you could rarely hear yourself think, let alone talk very much to someone else even if you wanted to pick them up. But there were times when you could sit down, have a drink and talk with someone for five or six minutes—by Studio standards, an "in depth" conversation! Sometimes you might be able to get together with a group of people you had met through mutual friends and stop for breakfast on the way home.

It was all pretty quick and fast, but for me, Studio 54 was a place of release. Bored and unchallenged as I might have been at ABT, during the week my life in the ballet was still regimented with class, rehearsals, performance, touring; like any dancer, I was always concerned about the placement of my body. At Studio 54 I could burst out in any direction, inventing whatever I wanted for myself. It was the grand finale of my week.

You'd lose every hang-up and inhibition you ever had, your paranoia in dealing with other people. You'd walk up to anyone, introduce yourself and start talking. You'd do things you'd never think of doing in a normal social setting. To a large extent, Studio 54 was so full of energy because of the drugs. They helped break down inhibitions. If I wanted to go to Studio 54 without drugs, I had to be in an extremely good mood and really want to be there. If I wasn't in a good mood and there were no drugs, I went home. I wasn't forced to do drugs, and I wasn't driven to drugs because of my problems. It wasn't that at all. I was clearly experimenting. I knew exactly what I was doing. Nearly everyone I knew in my generation experimented with drugs. In the late seventies it was nothing unusual. I was one of the fortunate people who found it possible to experiment with drugs and not get addicted and let them ruin my life.

After a while, I started to realize that the Studio 54 lifestyle bore little resemblance to reality. Trying to develop meaningful relationships was an exercise in futility. Most of the people I met there who were supposedly my friends, were merely acquaintances. I didn't really *know* them. It was very representative of New York. I meet hundreds of people on a regular basis. There are those I work with every day, those I meet in the dance world, those I meet socially, but there's only a handful of people I see, or even *want* to see, more than twice a week. Studio 54 magnified that aspect of New York life. Other than Gary, I hadn't initiated an important relationship through Studio in the three years I was going there. It started to make me think.

The first year I went to Studio 54, in 1977, I only went about four or five times. It steadily increased over the next two years to the point where, in the third year, I'd be going several times a week during layoffs. It was habit-forming, like a drug. In the beginning, every night was wild. Every night topped the last, until it eventually became passé. It wore thin. Finally, it hit me: I was addicted to Studio 54. It was 1979. When I wasn't at Studio, I *wanted* to be there, but when I got there, I began to have feelings of guilt and shame. Do I really want to be doing this five years from now? I wondered.

One summer night in 1979 before a planned trip to the beach, I asked Gary and his roommate Greg to come over to my apartment. Someone had given me something they called THC, a derivative of marijuana, and I asked Gary if he wanted to try some. Greg didn't do drugs, but Gary and I were both game for anything. I put out some "lines," Gary bent down and immediately snorted two of them. Following suit, I went down for mine and snorted one. I hadn't even finished, when I heard Gary call my name. Looking up, I saw his eyes bulging out of his head and he was gagging. He could hardly walk, but made it to the phone and called our friend Jack, but it was clear he couldn't relate to anything. "Why are we here on this

77

planet?" he asked no one in particular, then collapsed. Greg had to carry him home.

The drug was in my system, too. I was tripping. I lost all sense of depth perception, and my apartment seemed to disappear. It became a large void. Kenneth came home, and I didn't really know who he was. I didn't know what to do with myself. I felt claustrophobic, but the last thing I wanted to do was go outside. So I decided to take a bath. I got into the bath tub and couldn't feel the temperature of the water. I don't know how long I sat there, my thoughts splintered in a million disconnected directions, before I finally got out of the tub and went to bed, thinking, "If I can only go to sleep, this will all go away."

As I closed my eyes, I felt the bed tilt and turn into a big slide. I kept falling, falling, falling. . . . I had to keep opening my eyes to stop it. I had never been so frightened. But I finally drifted off to sleep. The next morning, I woke up with no apparent side effects, ready to go to the beach. I called Gary's house and my blood ran cold when Greg told me what had happened to Gary.

Greg put Gary to bed the minute they got home. At first, Gary's sensations of sinking, his body limbs growing and disconnecting, were similar to mine. Greg became frightened and not knowing what to do, called E. J., another friend who came over, and for a while Gary calmed down. But when they turned out the lights Gary's nightmare began. Legions of horrifying demons seemed to emerge from the walls, the bedclothes, and from within Gary's own body to devour him. For hours he fought them, trying to tell himself he was only tripping and tried to fall asleep. But, still awake as the sun came up, Gary heard the sounds of the city amplified in his mind until they were deafening. He felt his respiratory system begin to shut down. He managed to wake up Greg and tell him to take him to the hospital. He knew he was dying.

As they got out of a cab at Lenox Hill, Gary noticed a Christian Science church that reminded him of his Christian Science background and thought that if never before, this was the time to test the beliefs he had been brought up on. The doctor in the Emergency Room asked Gary what the problem was, and he told her he had taken THC. She looked him straight in the eye and said, "There's no such thing as THC, they don't make it anymore." She took his blood pressure and as matter-of-factly as possible said, "If you're heart doesn't stop beating that fast you're going to die." They took blood samples, and as he lay there, waiting for the results, Gary repeated his Christian Science prayers.

At this point, Gary remembers the kind of out of body experience, we now hear about from people who have died and come back. He crashed at the bottom of an abyss, then floated above his body. The sensation was ecstatic and he felt free to go on to the next plane of existence. Then, looking down at himself lying on the table, his griefstricken roommate at his side, he remembers thinking, "God, you're only 25 years old, and what a piece of baggage!" and accepted responsibility for the stupidity of putting into his body a substance he knew nothing about. He couldn't accept that. "Lisz, that's a cheap way to die, you were born for a better death than this," he thought. In a split second he felt himself zoom back into his body and convulse back to life. At that point the doctor walked back into the room and seeing Gary sitting up in bed, couldn't hide the amazement on her face. "Mr. Lisz," she said, "I can't understand how you've lived these eleven hours. You took a massive dose of *strychnine*."

I gave my best friend strychnine! The impact of those words slammed into my brain. It hadn't yet registered that I had taken it too, though a smaller dose. We heard later that strychnine is the "tripping" factor in LSD—acid—and the person who gave it to me forgot to tell us that we were only supposed to take a pinhead amount.

But the dosage wasn't the issue. What happened to us

79

scared me enough to stop taking drugs. Period. Period. Period. The excuse that we were young and not prepared to take responsibility for our own lives no longer rang true. Wanting to be "Children of the Night" at Studio 54 was clearly heading for a dead end. We finally realized that everything wasn't a big party. That party was over.

I didn't really have to think about the problem for very long. Having returned from the New York City Ballet, Mikhail Baryshnikov was named the new director of American Ballet Theatre and my focus turned completely around.

I don't think what I did in those three years was anything unusual for someone going through a period of frustration and self-doubt. Some people in similar situations withdraw, cutting themselves off from life, which is self-indulgent and self-destructive. I chose the opposite route, though equally indulgent and potentially destructive. But I wanted to see what was *out there,* in the world outside the ballet. With my situation at ABT, I was beginning to doubt that I wanted to be a professional ballet dancer. I wanted *success.*

I had thrown myself into the frenzied social whirl of Studio 54 and still maintained what was required of me as a corps de ballet dancer. Seeking the kind of approval socially that I wasn't receiving professionally, I was replacing one kind of fulfillment with another. By nature I have never been an addictive person when it comes to negative influences. But I can become addicted to anything positive—like friends, dancing and the theatre. When Misha took over ABT, it brought me back to the real reason I was in New York.

When Mikhail Baryshnikov came to America and joined ABT, he and Charles France became close friends. Despite being a Ph.D. candidate in French from Columbia, Charles found the ballet world irresistible and chose to take his chances there instead and had been working for ABT for twelve years. He worked his way up through the ranks from assisting in group sales, to assistant to ABT Co-director Oliver Smith, to the press office during the "Golden Years" of ABT, and became very well respected in the press world. On tour, he and Misha spent a lot of time together, often over several bottles of vodka. Charles was instrumental in introducing Misha to many aspects of American life, and of American dance in particular.

In 1975, Charles began working with Misha on Misha's personal narrative of his first two years of work in the West, *Baryshnikov at Work,* published in 1976. The dramatic black-and-white photographs were by Martha Swope. Charles was Editor and wrote the Introduction. When Misha became Artistic Director of American Ballet Theatre, he demonstrated his total confidence in Charles by appointing him Assistant to the Artistic Director.

With Misha now in charge of ABT, I needed to know if I could expect to advance more rapidly than I had under Lucia. I went to Charles and Florence Pettan, the ABT secretary, and told them that I felt I would have a better chance at a career if I went to Broadway.

They both felt I would be making a big mistake and that I should stay at ABT. Misha was intending to make a lot of changes, they said, and they told me he liked my dancing and wanted to help develop my talent. I believed them, since the only solo I had been given to that point was in his *Nutcracker.*

Prior to meeting Charles at that interview, I had only seen him once. It was during a *Bayadère* rehearsal. He was head of the press department at the time and I remember thinking that his large, "over-stuffed" frame was better suited to the world of opera than to ballet. He walked across the stage with a "Don't-fuck-with-me" attitude, and I noticed all the while that as his glasses constantly slipped down to the tip of his nose he'd repeatedly push them back up with one finger.

He was up front about everything and had a very regal manner that, at first, turned most people off, including myself. We would hear stories about his telling corps de ballet girls to lose weight, and if they tried to point out his size in return, he'd retort, "Well, my dear, I don't have to get out there on stage!" During my years in the corps de ballet, I didn't find Charles a very appealing person. But during our discussion about my career at ABT, I very quickly saw beyond the surface impression. I was intrigued by his intelligence, his taste, his wit, his attention to detail and I felt I could learn a great deal from him.

There are a lot of funny stories about dancers' contract discussions with management. For one, I heard that Dennis Wayne, when he was an ABT soloist, once tape-recorded his conversation with Lucia, during which she promised him a number of roles. When the year was over, he hadn't been given half those roles, and he wanted to sue the company.

Having heard this story, Peter Fonseca recorded his conversation with Misha. We learned very quickly that one of the new things about Misha's regime was that there *were* no promises! The new policy was to work as a member of the company by *dancing,* and when you were needed, you were needed. There were no more role negotiations.

Of course, at that point, I felt I had little to negotiate. I wanted a few solos here and there. I felt there were some roles I was very well suited for and should be dancing, such as one of the sailors in *Fancy Free.* I unquestionably had an affinity for that kind of dancing and I felt my onstage personality was right. At the time, there were dancers cast in *Fancy Free* who I felt shouldn't be dancing it. I thought I deserved a chance.

Florence and Charles did a lot of listening and said little. They did encourage me to stay on with the company, give myself time and perhaps something would happen. It was a hard decision, because all along, lurking in the back of my mind, was my childhood ambition to dance in Broadway musicals and perhaps eventually moving on to straight plays and films. It was very hard to prepare for those career choices and to be a ballet dancer at the same time. But deep down, I had a greater respect for ballet dancing. The technical demands and the scale of artistic dimensions were much more gratifying. I thought about it for about five minutes—and signed my contract. For the first time since joining ABT, I felt good about the people in charge. They were younger and had fresh ideas. Maybe, just maybe, I thought to myself, one of their ideas is to cast me in more ballets.

We came back from layoff, and already things had changed at ABT. The building where we had our studios on Sixty-first Street and Broadway had been demolished. Until our new facilities were ready, we rehearsed for six weeks at Radio City Music Hall. It was a rather comical period, American Ballet Theatre walking in the same stage door as the Rockettes! The company had a great sense of humor about it. I called my parents and told them I was now working at Radio City Music Hall. They had a good laugh.

There were more important changes at ABT. We started to rehearse a new production of the third act of *Raymonda,* which had lots of character dancing. Misha brought in one of his own teachers, Diana Joffe, a Latvian-born character-dance expert, to teach character class. Danish-born Stanley Williams, one of the world's most highly respected dance teachers, especially for men and the Bournonville style, was brought from the School of American Ballet to teach company class.

In the weeks at Radio City, I wasn't learning anything special. I decided it was best to bide my time during this transitional period, hoping that with the move to our new studios, my career would have a new beginning, too.

Chapter 8

THE waiting Charles France and Florence Pettan had advised me to do began to pay off in the fall of 1980. Soon after ABT moved from Radio City to the new studios at 890 Broadway at 19th Street, the rehearsal schedule for the upcoming season was posted, and I saw that for me, things were off to a flying start.

> *Thursday Oct. 30*
> 12:30-2:30   Prodigal Son
> 2:30-3:30   Prodigal Son
> 4:30-5:30   Giselle Peasant Pas Deux
> 5:30-7:30   Fancy Free
> *Friday Oct. 31* (Happy Halloween!!)
> 12:30-2:30   Prodigal Son
> 2:30-3:30   Prodigal Son
> 4:30-5:30   Prodigal Son
> 5:30-6:30   Raymonda (Czardas)
> 6:30-7:30   Rodeo
> *Saturday Nov. 1*
> 12:30-2:00   La Sonnambula (Harlequin)
> 2:00-3:00   Prodigal Son
> 4:30-5:30   Jardin aux Lilas
> 5:30-6:30   Interplay
> 6:30-7:30   Les Rendezvous (Pas de Trois)

I was finally going to have my chance to dance one of the Sailors in *Fancy Free,* a ballet I had been dying to do from the moment I first saw it. I was called to rehearsals along with Danilo Radojevic and Ronald Perry. Danny was cast as the swaggering show off, Ronald, the hot "Latin," and I was the shy romantic. Terry Orr was the balletmaster assigned to teach us the ballet. As a longtime principal with ABT, Terry had danced one of the Sailors in *Fancy Free* many times. When a dancer performs in a ballet over and over again through the years, he naturally gets to know the piece inside out, but it becomes very difficult to let go of the personal attachment to the ballet and view a new cast objectively.

Fancy Free requires a dynamic sense of camaraderie among the three sailors and, other than on a working basis, Danny, Ronald and I hardly knew each other. It was a definite struggle for us to discover how to convey a feeling of genuine friendship right off the bat. That element of friendship was all there, built into the choreography, but it wouldn't be convincing unless we found a way to make the gestures come from within ourselves. It wasn't something we could put on like our sailor suits. It would take time and a lot of work. Understandably, Terry had trouble accepting the absence of a quality he had come to take for granted over the years. So it was rough going for the three of us trying to achieve exactly what Terry was accustomed to seeing. At times, rehearsals got very tense.

Misha, who had danced in *Fancy Free* during his time with the New York City Ballet, asked Jerry Robbins to come to rehearsals toward the end of the rehearsal period. He actually said very little, but at the time I suspected Jerry felt the ballet had somehow gotten out of his hands, and he didn't really have the time to fine tune the ballet on a day-to-day basis the way he could with the NYCB production. The cast, which also included my friends Elaine Kudo and Kelley Hughes as the two lead girls, were rather let down that Jerry seemed so unenthusiastic. As it turned out, he had either liked us from the beginning, or felt that we had improved a great deal, because a year later he brought the same cast to the Festival of Two Worlds in Spoleto, Italy, to perform *Fancy Free* on all-Robbins program that included *New York Export: Opus Jazz, Afternoon of a Faun,* and *Other Dances.* After numerous performances on tour, the brilliant theatrical nuances of Jerry's choreography became second nature to the cast members. Danny, Ronald and I gradually developed that dynamic sense of camaraderie on stage—but we still never went out together at night after a performance to drink beer and chase girls!

Rodeo, Agnes de Mille's classic Americana ballet about a young woman who wants to be "one of the boys" but gets her man only when she becomes "one of the girls," was another of those ballets I felt well-suited to. I was called to rehearsals for the Champion Roper, the guy the girl gets, with Ruth Mayer as the Cow Girl. I felt that Ruth, with her exquisitely patrician features and long, iridescent red hair, was much too beautiful for the role of the plain tomboy, but being one of the great dance actresses of our generation, she could portray a lily pad on a pond if you asked her. I'm sure that's why Agnes de Mille liked casting Ruth in her ballets ("The Mother" in *Fall River Legend,* the "Lusty One" in *Three Virgins and a Devil*), and wanted her for *Rodeo.*

Having made a miraculous recovery from a debilitating stroke several years earlier, Agnes de Mille emanated a still powerful pride and determined will as she walked into the rehearsal room, assisted by a young woman. But when I went up to greet her, this matriarch of American dance, preferring to be escorted by a young gentleman, immediately took my arm. As we walked to her chair, I noticed that no one else in the room was moving. The dancers stood there in silent anticipation of what she would say, as if awaiting a pronouncement by the Oracle at Delphi.

Actually, Agnes de Mille *is* somewhat an oracle of American dance. In the rehearsals that followed, she was extremely verbal, always articulate. She spent a great deal of time describing each of the roles, often asking us what we, as our characters, would do in any given situation. She wanted us to *be* those characters. If we were called upon to "ride horses," we had to be *riding horses,* not miming them. "Have you ever ridden a horse?" she'd ask a young corps dancer. If he shook his head, "No," she'd snap, "Well, go ride one!"

Being a self-professed historian, Agnes didn't ignore any resource that might help us understand the ballet. At one point, she brought in authentic pictures of real cowboys, the type of thing you'd see in *American Heritage.* To me, they just looked like old cowboys, but I understood and appreciated the intention.

I felt I was a good choice for the Champion Roper. I was still rather young, but the tap solo required in the role was a natural for me considering my early dance background. And I *was* from Texas. I can't exactly say that I was "born in the saddle" (I was thrown the first time I ever got on a horse), but I certainly knew the feeling and growing up had seen enough real bow-legged cowhands to know what she was asking for.

Agnes had one especially irritating habit. She'd lean on her cane, watching rehearsals with an eagle eye, then suddenly, without warning, she'd bang on the mirror with this monster ring she wore on her left hand. The piercing sound was totally unnerving. It got our attention all right! Even in the midst of the most chaotic rehearsals, we'd stop dead in our boots.

Balletmaster Terry Orr, who had performed a memorably strutting and feisty Champion Roper, taught us the ballet. As rehearsals progressed during the four week rehearsal period, Ruth and I realized we had to fight the images of the Cow Girl and Champion Roper the public, and even we ourselves, had come to expect. Certain dancers had been identified with the leading roles over the years, especially Christine Sarry, as the Cow Girl, and William Carter, as the Champion Roper. With her short, angular body and pixie haircut, Christine *looked* like a tomboy, plain and simple, and when she made her entrance wearing a dress for the ranch house dance, you truly believed she'd never worn a dress before in her life. It left an indelible comic impression. Bill Carter, one of America's great character dancers and master of many dance styles (ballet, modern, tap, Spanish), gave the role an inimitable masculine warmth and vulnerability. He gave the Champion Roper "heart."

Ruth's Cow Girl was more feminine and contemporary. She wanted her equality with men accepted as a woman, not as "one of the boys." When I would stagger back at the sight of her wearing a dress, it wasn't so much because she looked comical as it was due to my sudden realization of the foolishness of thinking she needed to put on a dress in order to be accepted. It made the ballet something more of a statement on the outdated prejudices of men, which I believe has always been a valid interpretation. As the Champion Roper, I more or less took my lead from Ruth's characterization. I was just a young, regular kind of guy looking for the ideal woman. At first attracted by the obvious feminine appeal of the Ranch Owner's Daughter, I ultimately acted on my better judgment, saw Ruth's Cow Girl for the genuine and forthright person she was and fell for her.

It was an odd experience to realize how *difficult* it was to cast aside our stereotyped images of the roles and feel comfortable in the portrayals we knew were most natural to us. But after long and hard work in rehearsals, believing that Agnes de Mille knew what she was doing by casting us, and through repeated performances on tour, Ruth and I overcame our misgivings and "lived it up." Performing the Champion Roper in *Rodeo* taught me an important lesson: an artist doesn't need to be held to or intimidated by the accepted or traditional interpretations of any given role. You can't go out on stage and be another dancer, nor should you attempt or expect to. Dancers are not impersonators. The only thing you can do when you're dancing a role that is associated with another dancer is to do something completely individual—force the viewer to re-evaluate that role. Of course having to work with a good strong ballet that can withstand any number of valid interpretations, like *Rodeo*, doesn't hurt!

When the rehearsal schedule went up for the ABT premiere of Balanchine's *Prodigal Son*, four names were listed for learning the title role, Misha (who had already danced it with NYCB), Danilo Radojevic, George de la Peña . . . and myself. I found it hard to believe. Throughout the rehearsal period, I never thought I would get to dance *Prodigal ever*, let alone that season.

Misha was teaching at the time, and he was putting great emphasis on the importance of taking company class. In the past members of the company often took classes with teachers at studios elsewhere around New York, or did their own barre, and seldom took company class. He was enforcing a stricter daily routine and I usually took his class. But at one point in the middle of the week when I started rehearsing *Prodigal*, I got very sore and decided to warm up by doing my own barre in the other studio.

Misha taught that day and after class stormed into the room. It was the first time I had ever seen him really angry. "Robby! How do you expect to dance a role like Prodigal Son if you don't take class?" he shouted like a father reprimanding a naughty child.

I was dumbfounded. I couldn't understand what I had done to deserve his attack. What was I doing wrong? In my mind I got defensive, thinking, One day of not taking class, and this is what I get! He turned and stormed out of the room. It suddenly dawned on me that Misha was upset because he cared very much about my artistic development and my future.

Also, he was trying to make a bigger point—it was not simply that I had missed class that particular day. He wanted to stress the importance of taking class *every* day as a matter of self-discipline, no matter how you felt. And he was right. Later on, as my professional career advanced, it became next to nothing for me to go to class. It became a habitual, unconscious part of my routine. When I was in the corps, I didn't need to take class every day. But as you take on soloist or principal roles, you have to come into the studio really warm because you can injure yourself horribly. As you get older it's a lot more difficult to rehearse when your muscles are cold. The physical demands become much greater and you have to be warmed up in order to execute what you need to do.

So, rehearsals went on, and John Taras, one of Balanchine's long-standing New York City Ballet ballet masters, was teaching *Prodigal.* Since he had been so closely associated with Balanchine's ballet for so many years, he knew how it should look. My image of the role was not at all well defined, since I had only seen it once with Edward Villella. I retained certain images of it, like the famous jumping over the fence, the "goons" and the crawling home to the father. That was about all I could remember.

Everything else was very new to me. For the first time, I wasn't learning a ballet that I had seen other dancers do in recent memory, and found it very challenging to rely solely on the ballet-master to get me to produce what he knew. John kept shouting very loudly in rehearsal to get a certain kind of anger out of me. At first I didn't understand why he wanted me to be angry. He was trying to produce the image of a young boy who was so frustrated with his life that he wanted to leave home. This first dance had to be very powerful, almost barbaric, with clenched fists, flexed muscles, and jabbing leaps. Of course John made frequent references to Eddie Villella, to his powerful jump, the attack of his steps and his musculature.

So, through much of this, I didn't understand why I was

91

learning the part. I was still rather slight, but taller and thinner, basically the opposite type from Eddie, who was short, compactly muscular and very Mediterranean-looking.

It was difficult to understand why I had been cast. But at the same time, I knew it could be a very big break in my career if I ever got to do a performance.

John, and later Misha, kept demonstrating things like beating your thigh, struggling away from your sisters, and constantly running around with an open mouth and a hand gesture to the mouth that suggests a scream. Those were very verbal rehearsals, because John tried to produce a certain quality that couldn't be learned in a classroom. I caught on to the choreography, but I didn't really *understand* what I was doing. I was just doing steps and trying to make sense out of it.

After the fourth day of rehearsals, we started learning the scene with the drinking companions, the goons. That scene made perfect sense to me. I could relate with the Prodigal's insatiable curiosity. It was not unlike the point I was at in my own life. I had already experienced something like the opening scene earlier in life. I didn't feel Prodigal's *anger*, necessarily, but, always eager as a boy to get away from Beaumont, I identified with the frustration of feeling the need to leave home. But the next scene was very easy because from step to step you had to communicate with the other characters, your two friends and the goons, these eight weird guys wearing bald wigs and black veins all over their bodies. It's like the scene from the movie *Star Wars* that takes place in the bar patronized by bizarre aliens. So, there's an overriding feeling of curiosity, wanting to know what life has in store. The goons offer the Prodigal a drink, and he takes it. They want to take the jewels from his clothes, so he shares his possessions with them. It's an action scene I could relate to very easily.

Then in comes the Siren, a tall seductress with a very long, burgundy red cape trailing behind her. Her steps involve twisting the cape through her legs into a rather vulgar suggestion of a woman having her period. It's very grotesque and racy at the same time, especially considering it was created in 1929. I'm sure it must have been shocking for its time. For the Prodigal, it's the very first time he's seen a woman display herself in this manner. Naturally, he's curious.

When I first started to rehearse with the ballerina, Cynthia Gregory, I couldn't believe that I was actually going to touch this woman in a professional way. I never thought that I would ever actually get a chance to dance with her. I had always thought that by the time that I started to progress in the company, if I indeed ever *did* start to progress, Cynthia would have left ABT. I also thought that I was too short to dance with her. However, *Prodigal Son* requires a tall woman and a shorter man, so we were physically right for it. Cynthia has this amazing gift of learning a ballet at a very, very advanced pace. She must have had to learn quickly in her childhood, because it's very second nature to her.

It was interesting that from the first rehearsal her character was almost fully developed. She understood the role as though Mr. Balanchine had made it for her. When we finally performed it together, I noticed that there was little difference in her performance from that first rehearsal to the onstage performance, because she started on such a high level. Cynthia always came into a rehearsal room with an eagerness and willingness to learn. She knew she could stand up literally on her own two feet, or one, if necessary, whenever she had to. She was so strong, she needed very little partnering help from me.

We started our work on the pas de deux, which is all about her seduction of the Prodigal. He puts one hand on her stomach, and another on her breast. She takes it off, then pushes his head into her breasts. She exposes her leg and, as the Prodigal reaches for it, pulls it away at the last moment. She tempts him with every inch of her being. Cynthia's Siren

wasn't evil. She was very, very sexy. I had never seen Cynthia
be so blatantly sexual. Cynthia's onstage image was always
regal or distinguished. In my mind, this was a fascinating new
persona for her. It was so erotic. We learned the pas de deux
very quickly, and it was a challenge to keep up with her.

After the pas de deux, the drinking companions return.
They ply the Prodigal with drink and play around with him,
at one point carrying him overhead like a conquering hero.
But their play turns malicious; they throw him around
viciously, tear his clothes and steal his possessions. They fling
him against a wall and run away. Even his two best friends
desert him.

I next learned my favorite part, the wonderful moment
where the Prodigal, beaten and alone, realizes he has nothing
left in life but to try to return home. His energy is sapped, he
has no muscular sensation, he fears his eyesight is failing. He
has barely enough strength to cup his hands in order to drink
some water. He struggles to stand and falls. He sees people
along the way on the journey, and asks for help and they turn
away. Naked and covered with dirt, he feels like a leper. This
is one of the great acting scenes in ballet. Nothing I'd learned
in all my training at the ballet barre could be called upon to
get me through it. In fact, from that moment on in the *Prodigal
Son*, there's no "dancing" left. I was basically on my knees
crawling.

Misha came into rehearsal to help with this section. He
demonstrated what he had done in the New York City Ballet
production. It's funny that in a rehearsal room, when dancers
are doing a dramatic scene where there's very little technical
dance, they rarely do it full out, the way I assume actors
would rehearse. Maybe actors don't do it exactly the way
they will perform the role onstage, but they certainly don't
mark it. But I remember Misha coming in and showing me the
whole last section, demonstrating to heartbreaking perfection
the pure and simple need to crawl home.

Because several casts were learning *Prodigal Son,* it still hadn't been decided who would dance it with whom. I didn't even know if I would do it at all, since final casting hadn't gone up. I had some rehearsals with Martine van Hamel and some with Magali Messac. With Martine, the Siren is a very different woman. There was another kind of sexual tension there. She approached it a little more like the madam of a brothel. I think her interpretation was a little older and more worldly. Her Siren had been through a lot more than Cynthia's. It was sensuous in a more hardened, almost masculine, way, but never rough.

The experience of working with Megali Messac was different again. She has a mole in the center of her forehead that makes her look extremely exotic in an Oriental sense, even though she's French. So, with her it was truly like going off to a foreign country and seeing something I'd never seen before in my life. I was fascinated by the unfamiliar. Megali played the Siren as a very beautiful woman. She approached the pas de deux not so much as a seduction than as a matter of mutual attraction.

A week before the scheduled premiere in Washington, the final casting still hadn't gone up. One afternoon, between my rehearsals, Charles called me into his office.

"Sit down, Robby," he said. "I've got something to tell you." I walked slowly into the room, and sat down nervously, wondering if I had done something wrong. "Misha has decided he wants you to dance the opening night performance of *Prodigal*—with Cynthia as your Siren!" he continued, barely able to contain his own excitement. I was in total shock. I couldn't find the words to respond.

Seeing me dumbfounded, Charles was rather pleased with himself for being the bearer of this sensational news. "Okay. You've got your work cut out for you," he chuckled, "now go *do* it!"

I got up, went to the door, and left, without having said a

95

word the entire time. When I found out, I was naturally elated, but also scared. It was a very big jump from having done just a few solo parts in *Nutcracker* and demi-solos in *Don Quixote,* to a role that required someone with a great deal of experience. I knew that no matter how much rehearsal time I got, only performance experience was going to make me understand more about the role and develop the character. I had the feeling that this role would either make or break my chances of ever having a career as a principal dancer.

Misha was very excited about my doing the Prodigal. He invited me to his apartment to see the videotape of his performance as the Prodigal, which Balanchine had coached him in for PBS. It was a Sunday, our day off. He had this beautiful apartment on Park Avenue, the kind you would imagine a famous person would have, with beautiful antiques, lots of books and a dog. It made me a fan all over again. I couldn't believe I was going over to Mikhail Baryshnikov's house to watch his video of *Prodigal Son.* We saw the video, then sat and talked about it. He didn't say that much as far as coaching me. He allowed me the freedom to take from it what I saw for myself. However, he did mention a few images that Mr. Balanchine had explained to him.

Misha told me how "Mr. B" had described the opening of the pas de deux. In Balanchine's words, the position of the bodies in the moment when the Siren and the Prodigal fall sensuously toward each other from opposite sides of the stage as if they were drawn by sexual magnetism should be, "You know, dear, like Russian icons." It brought to mind the huge Russian icons in Jerome Robbins's *Les Noces,* and I immediately understood the flattened, two-dimensional image he was asking for.

Balanchine had changed some things choreographically only for the film, Misha continued. Things were done differently for reasons of spacing, musicality, and because certain camera angles would emphasize and clarify aspects of the ballet that could not be brought out on stage. The whole time we sat there, I tried to absorb everything Misha was telling me. But somewhere in the back of my mind, I still had trouble believing that I, Robert La Fosse, a kid from Beaumont, Texas, was sitting with the greatest dancer of our time discussing *my* debut in George Balanchine's masterpiece, *Prodigal Son*.

At the end of the New York rehearsal period, we did what are called complete run-throughs. Everyone seemed pleased. But no matter how pleased the ballet-masters and directors are, the audience and critics must still be faced. My biggest fear about the performance was the thought of being onstage with a great artist and star like Cynthia Gregory. I was afraid that next to hers, my performance would look amateurish.

I had made a point of not looking at any films of Edward Villella in the role or doing any other sort of comparative research. My only frame of reference was Misha's performance on tape. I assumed that although I wanted it to be completely original, my interpretation was going to be along the same lines.

We flew to Washington, and shortly before the opening came the scandal over the firing of Gelsey Kirkland and Patrick Bissell. Apparently it was due to the fact that they had missed their flight to Washington and had also missed a rehearsal of *Pas d'Esclave*, which they were scheduled to dance opening night. Consequently, Susan Jaffe, whose career was about to parallel my own, was snatched out of the corps de ballet to replace Gelsey in *Pas d'Esclave*, and her partner would be Russian star Alexander Godunov, in his ABT debut. At the time, I thought it was outrageous on the part of the management. It was known in the company that they did drugs, but everyone had their own moral standards, and as long as a dancer showed up for rehearsal and did his or her job, what they do in their personal lives is nobody's business. It's almost impossible to approach a fellow company member who has a drinking or drug problem about his or her problem, no matter how much one cares for the person. There simply are certain lines we usually don't cross. It was common knowledge about Gelsey's and Patrick's problems throughout the rehearsal period, but I don't think anyone said anything directly to them.

At the time, Misha was trying to make the transition with the company from fellow dancer to Artistic Director, and there were dancers who tested him. Some principal dancers wanted to have the same control over him that they had had over Lucia. They could go into Lucia, demand things and usually get them. Already the principal dancers' salaries had been cut back from a per-performance basis to a weekly salary. Needless to say, this didn't go over too well.

But the Kirkland/Bissell controversy was something completely different. At one point, a Washington reporter asked me what I thought about Gelsey and Patrick being fired. My naive response was that I didn't know why it had happened, but the action sounded a little rash to me, and Misha should have given them another chance. Not knowing the details, as most of us didn't, that's how it looked to us. I myself was an innocent bystander, and didn't know how serious their drug problem was or what they were going through. My comment appeared in the newspaper, and seeing my quote in print didn't please me too much. I didn't like having anything I said repeated when I really didn't know that much about the situation. At the time, I was sympathetic to Gelsey and Patrick as dancers. Had I known the truth about what was going on and been in Misha's position, I probably would have fired them too.

Opening night came, and the curtain at the Kennedy Center went up. I had been rehearsing all day long for other ballets in addition to a two-hour stage rehearsal for *Prodigal*, which I did full out. I was already tired before I did a step. But no matter how weary you are, a good case of stage fright charges you with a million volts of electricity. It makes you feel like going for another week without sleep.

I made my entrance and started the first step in the "dance of anger." But I was so caught up in the character and what he was trying to say, that I completely blanked out. Despite all the rehearsals for this variation, which is not even a minute long, I couldn't remember a step! I instinctively made up some choreography for about eight counts, until I snapped out of it and found my place in the music. That momentary lapse scared me so much, I forgot what I had been scared about to begin with. This freed me to concentrate on what I was doing, trying to keep my head above water, and do justice to the role.

Once relaxed, I was able to settle into the rest of the performance without needing that edge of stage fright. I knew by the end of the pas de deux with Cynthia, that things were going well because the audience reception was truly extraordinary. It encouraged me enough to continue in the direction I was going. A dancer on stage can always sense what the audience is feeling. Even silence can tell you that you're holding their attention. You can feel it as a performer—and that helps you to carry on.

By the time I got to the part where the goons beat up the Prodigal and throw him against the wall, I wasn't acting at all. I had been so tired from rehearsing all day that when I sank down to my knees, pleading for help, it was the furthest thing from an acting job. It was real. I had immersed myself in the situation, and I was truly exhausted.

At the moment where the Father comes from the tent to accept the Prodigal back into the family fold, he raises his arm in a gesture to call his son to him, rather than his going to the son. Seeing the Father's gesture, the Prodigal gets scared, frightened that he's offended him too deeply to be forgiven. Yet, the Prodigal must atone for his sin. It's a moment of great humiliation and embarrassment. Clutching the fence, I started to weep. I don't know whether it was due to the inherent drama of that moment in the ballet, or because I was so tired and relieved finally to have made it to that point, but the tears were something that I didn't rehearse or plan. It was also partly a feeling of knowing I had done well for myself, that I had delivered the kind of performance that I had hoped to deliver.

The Prodigal must then crawl across the stage on his knees, his hands held together behind his back as if bound at the wrists. Weighed down with shame, I groveled across the stage, clutched my Father's robes, and crawled up his body and into his arms, and the curtain fell.

The reception was enormous. I had never felt appreciation like that from any person or event. One of the best sensations in life is not only to *hear*, but to *feel* thousands of people applauding. They're grateful to you. You're grateful to them. It's an almost spiritual experience. I took my bows and was so emotionally involved and overwhelmed, I cried again. These were tears of joy. I realized how truly tears were a physical manifestation of the feeling that you are loved.

Chapter 9

WHEN Gelsey Kirkland came back to the company after one of her several hiatuses, she needed ballets to dance that were on the easy side. Management struggled to find a repertoire that would be not only suitable, but comfortable for her, given her well-known difficulties in rehearsing five or six ballets at a time. Furthermore, Misha intended to dance with her as little as possible, and the other principal male dancers, with the exception of Kevin McKenzie and myself, followed suit. Gelsey was scheduled to dance the pas de deux in *Great Galloping Gottschalk* that Lynne Taylor-Corbett created on Susan Jaffe and me.

Having danced with Gelsey in a performance of *Giselle* in Long Island for Edward Villella, I knew what she was like to work with. Her obsession with being a perfectionist at the expense of other dancers, her need to rehearse excessively to the point where every detail was so calculated that there was no spontaneity left, her difficulty in explaining herself, in communicating. I knew all of it and I wasn't terribly excited about dancing with her.

I like to get out on stage and discover aspects of a role through performing it. I save things for the stage. Gelsey is the opposite. Hers is definitely a calculated performance. I'm the first to admit it doesn't *look* like that to the audience, but it is. We started the rehearsals, and coming from New York City Ballet, she learned very quickly. However, that first day we couldn't even get beyond the first step because she wanted to perfect it. At one point, we got so bogged down I finally had to plead with her to just get on with it, learn the whole pas de deux and then go back and clean things up later. If not, we were never going to learn the whole pas de deux.

I didn't know for sure at the time, but it appeared to me that she was still doing drugs. In fact, no one knew for sure. Looking back on it now, even if we had known, there was nothing anyone could do about it. It's clearly up to the individual to get help. As I've said, confrontations in such cases are very difficult, especially in a working situation. I wasn't particularly friendly with Gelsey—it was solely a working relationship—so I couldn't have said anything.

In any case, she would often come to rehearsals ten or fifteen minutes late, wearing the same clothes, the same outfit, almost every day. She would wear pointe shoes that were so broken in that it was dangerous for her to dance in them. Extremely soft shoes, providing little or no support, are very hard on the feet. Gelsey always had a very, very powerful presence. She wasn't very friendly. She never went out of her way to please people. It was evident to me that she clearly didn't *care* about pleasing other people. She seemed concerned about pleasing herself. I think this contributed to her powerful persona. No one really knew Gelsey very well. There weren't that many people who were close to her. She simply didn't allow people to get close.

Lynne Taylor-Corbett was very helpful to Gelsey in rehearsals. She tried not to spoil her. She would show Gelsey the steps, or I would show her what Susan Jaffe had originally done. For the most part, that experience went pretty smoothly. It was the first ballet Gelsey was going to dance on her return to ABT, and I felt she was determined to convince people that she truly wanted to come back. We rehearsed an

102

awful lot. We needed to because Gelsey didn't allow herself to be the naturally gifted dancer she is. In this case, since the choreography was more modern in style, she had to analyze the weight changes, the contractions and the way the torso leads the whole body. It appeared that dancing was a science to her more than an artistic self-expression. But then again, just the fact that she was going to be back on the stage was a triumph for her at that point.

When Gelsey and I started rehearsals for Balanchine's *La Sonnambula,* the first rehearsal we had was with John Taras. He had been a ballet-master with the New York City Ballet for many years and had known Gelsey when she was there. From the outset, there was a lot of tension in the room. John didn't give Gelsey preferential treatment and had no second thoughts about correcting her on certain steps, explaining what Mr. Balanchine wanted.

At one point, Gelsey got very pissed off. I don't know if she was high or not, but she got very mad at John and started to mock him by doing a caricatured imitation of the stereotypical Balanchine dancer. It was completely uncalled for and didn't get anyone anywhere. I didn't understand what an artist like Gelsey had to prove by behaving like that and wondered where she thought it would get her. John, normally an exceptionally patient ballet master, finally got so fed up he said, "Well, Gelsey, you can just dance it anyway you want," and left the room.

The next day, Georgina Parkinson, the former Royal Ballet ballerina who was now an ABT ballet mistress, took the rehearsal for the pas de deux. I was there for the one o'clock rehearsal and Georgina and I started talking. Ten minutes went by, and we assumed that Gelsey would be coming in her usual fifteen minutes late. We talked a little more. Still no Gelsey. I went to the office and asked where Gelsey was, and no one seemed to know. I told them I would wait five more minutes. I went back to the rehearsal room and resumed the conversation. By this time twenty minutes had gone by, and we really didn't care any longer if she showed up or not. We were past the point of even getting annoyed.

At one-thirty, Gelsey ambled in. She didn't say she was sorry for being late and seemed to be very high. She probably didn't even realize she was late. She walked to the center of the room, ready to start working. I couldn't believe what I was about to do, but I picked up my dance bag and walked to the door and said, "The next time you're late, Gelsey, I think you should at least have the courtesy to call and let Georgina, the pianist and myself know. We have better things to do than sit around waiting for you. It's very rude." And I walked out.

I went directly to the office and told Misha, "Misha, I just walked out on Gelsey. She was thirty minutes late." That was the last I heard of it. I wasn't trying to be nasty. I felt I couldn't let Gelsey get away with treating people that way. Whatever trip she was on, whether it was cocaine or a star trip, it was a *bad habit.* I can't respect anyone, no matter who they are, who behaves that way. It's totally unprofessional. So, I made a choice I believed in by walking out on her.

The next day, she came up to me and apologized. I told her to her face that she just couldn't expect people to wait on her and ignore such inconsiderate treatment. She agreed and promised it would never happen again. Sure enough, the next day she was her usual ten or fifteen minutes late. Nothing changed. She was always ready with excuses about how much she had to do or something equally vague. What made matters worse was that not only did we start late, but we'd rehearse for fifteen minutes and she'd have to go running to the bathroom. She'd come back with a glazed look in her eyes and her skin would have this kind of neon glow to it.

To say the least, it was disappointing for me to have such trouble working with Gelsey. She had always been my favorite ballerina but, unwittingly and helpless to stop herself, seemed hell-bent on wrenching the stars from my eyes. But I learned a lot. In one of the last rehearsals we had for *Sonnambula,* we were working on the end of the pas de deux. There is a moment at the end of the pas de deux where the Poet stops the Sleepwalker by the shoulders, kisses her and she floats away back into the tower. For that one four seconds of time, Gelsey insisted that we spend an entire hour working on the technique of how to kiss. Her version was calculated and studied. What she was trying to say during that hour was that when we kissed, she didn't want our kiss to come from the lips. She wanted it to emanate through our chests from our hearts and our souls. Essentially it was all in the placement of my neck. Instead of jutting my neck out forward and pursing my lips to kiss her, she wanted me to keep my neck up straight so that our bodies would come together. But she really couldn't explain herself that well. She would get so excited about it, that she'd start screaming from the frustration of trying to convey what she meant. I became completely wrapped up in it. I tried to understand what she was saying, for her sake, and wanted to learn something from her. But it was also a little absurd—working an hour on a four-second kiss when it could have been done honestly and sincerely and have had just the same effect.

It was especially difficult to feel motivated after a while, considering her disheveled appearance and the sight of her pouting lips unattractively distorted by silicon. I was trying to be patient, but by the twenty-fifth try, with some that she liked and others that she didn't, and not really knowing which was which, I had gotten to the point where I was completely frustrated with myself for not being able to please her. "Gelsey," I said, tears burning my eyes, "I'm just so afraid I won't be able to do what you want, that you'll give up on me." Then I started to cry.

Seeing that she had brought a grown man to the point of tears, she comforted me. It was the first time I had ever seen her show concern for someone else.

Although I grew to hate every moment of those rehearsals, I had learned something from working with an artist whose onstage work I admired. I discovered something extraordinary about Gesley in working with her on *La Sonnambula*: She had grown up watching Allegra Kent as the mysterious Sleepwalker in the New York City Ballet production, and couldn't get that image out of her mind. It was understandable, since Allegra Kent, one of Balanchine's most legendary ballerinas, has been most closely identified with *La Sonnambula* for decades. Everything she ever talked about was related to Allegra, saying, "When Allegra did this," and "When Allegra did that. . . ." It seemed to me that she was trying to recapture the exact memory of what Allegra had looked like and strived to transform herself into that. I felt that was very restricting. Yet, despite her obsession with recreating Allegra Kent's interpretation, on stage Gelsey magically made the role one hundred per cent her own. It's an artistic achievement that I've never seen work for anyone else. I also recognized through this experience that I, for right or wrong, would put myself into any situation, no matter how difficult, to please others.

Portrait of a young ABT—(l to r) Raymond Serrano, Fanchon Cordell, Peter Fonseca, Elaine Kudo, Robert LaFosse, Lisa Rinehart. (Photo by Max Waldman)

In Jerome Robbins' *Fancy Free*, with Danilo Radojevic (left) and Ronald Perry (right). (Photo by Mira)

In Antony Tudor's *Jardin aux Lilas*, with, l to r: Martine van Hamel, Leslie Browne, and Erich Weichardt. (Photo by Martha Swope)

Rehearsing the "Champion Roper" in Agnes de Mille's *Rodeo*, 1982. (Photo by Sue Martin)

In the "Pas de Trois" from Sir Frederick Ashton's *Les Rendezvous*, with Gregory Osborne and Lisa de Ribere. (Photo by Martha Swope)

In Jerome Robbins' *N.Y. Export: Opus Jazz*, 1983. (Photo by Sue Martin)

With Susan Jaffe in *Opus Jazz*.
(Photo by Martha Swope)

Coached by choreographer Lynn Taylor Corbett, in rehearsal with Susan
Jaffe for *Great Galloping Gottschalk*, 1981. (Photo by Reed Jenkins)

With Susan Jaffe in performance of *Great Galloping Gottschalk*. (Photo by Mira)

As the ''Wild Boy'' with (l to r) Brian Adams, Natalia Makarova, Ross Stretton, in Kenneth MacMillan's *The Wild Boy*, 1982. (Photo by Sue Martin)

The "Wild Boy." (Photo by Sue Martin)

With Mikhail Baryshnikov rehearsing John McFall's *Follow the Feet*, 1983.
(Photo by Martha Swope)

Lifting Misha in that "tricky lift" in *Follow the Feet*, 1983. (Photo by Sue Martin)

My favorite lift with Misha in *Follow the Feet*, 1983.
(Photo by Martha Swope)

As "Hilarion,"
with Gelsey Kirland
as "Giselle,"
in *Giselle, Act I*.
(Photo by Mira)

As the "Poet" with Gelsey Kirkland as the "Sleepwalker" in the ABT
production of Balanchine's *La Sonnambula*, 1983. (Photo by Martha Swope)

As "Albrecht," with Cynthia Harvey as "Giselle," in *Giselle, Act I.* (Photo by Mira)

As "James," with Cynthia Harvey as the "Sylph," in *La Sylphide, Act I.*
(Photo by Martha Swope)

Performing James's solo
in *La Sylphide, Act I.*
(Photo by Martha
Swope)

As "James," with Gelsey
Kirkland as the "Sylph," in
La Sylphide, Act II (1984)
(Photo by Sue Martin)

As an "Ugly Stepsister" (at left), with Megali Messac ("Cinderella") and
Victor Barbee (the other "Ugly Sister") in the Anastos/Baryshnikov
Cinderella, 1983. (Photo by Martha Swope)

At the ball, as the "Ugly Stepsister" (on pointe) and . . . (photo by Martha Swope)

. . . as the "Prince" with Marianna Tcherkassky as "Cinderella." (Photo by Sue Martin)

In a lighter moment during rehearsals for Sir Kenneth MacMillan's *Romeo and Juliet*, with (l to r) Sir Kenneth MacMillan, Victor Barbee ("Tybalt") and Danilo Radojevic ("Mercutio"). (Photo by Martha Swope)

A more serious moment in rehearsal with Victor Barbee, as (center, l to r) ballet masters Terry Orr and David Richardson and Sir Kenneth, look on. (Photo by Martha Swope)

As Romeo with Elaine Kudo in *Romeo and Juliet, Act. I.* (Photo by Martha Swope)

As Romeo with Elaine Kudo and Danilo Radojevic in *Romeo and Juliet*, Act I. (Photo by Martha Swope)

Romeo meets Juliet (Leslie Browne) at the Capulet's ball. (Photo by Martha Swope)

With Leslie Browne as Shakespeare's star-crossed lovers. (Photo by Martha Swope)

Chapter 10

BECAUSE the dance world is so small, everyone seems to find out, or think they find out, everything about everybody, critics included. Sometimes I'm sure they find it difficult to evaluate separately what they see going on onstage from what they hear is going on backstage. You have to wonder how much a negative review might have been influenced by what the writer has heard about the dancer's private life—in my case, my friendship with Charles France, Misha's assistant director.

Charles and I became friends. As I got to know him better, I realized what an amazing person he is and found myself seeking out his company, to hear more about his early education and traveling experiences in Europe, things that were totally foreign to anything I had known as a child. We didn't just talk about ballet, we'd discuss art, literature, people. Much of my friendship with Charles was a learning experience that filled me in on many of the things I had missed in school. He was easy to be around because he had no trouble being with a dancer and a younger person at that. We got along very well. We had a lot of things in common. Like me, Charles had studied ballet as a youngster. We had similar tastes. We loved musical theatre, plays, films, antiques. We're both from the South; he's from Oklahoma and I'm from Texas. Many of our attitudes about life are the same. Our friendship developed quite naturally and unconsciously. I never foresaw anything negative coming from it.

It was not until much later that I began to hear rumors and misconceptions about our relationship. It woke me up to the fact that perhaps befriending someone in "the management" wasn't standard procedure. But that's the nature of rumors. Rumors are about the way people *want* things to look, not the way they are.

Charles was a great friend not only to me, but to most of the dancers in the company. He was always very concerned about the way people looked onstage and if they needed more rehearsal time, he saw to it that they did it. He encouraged all the dancers in the company to work better in class and in rehearsals.

Someone has to look after the dancers, to see that they have enough preparation before going on stage. That's where Charles is such an enormous help. He looks after everyone. If Misha cast someone in a role, Charles knew the dancer well enough to know what was needed to make that performance the best possible. This isn't to say that Charles isn't always tactful. He's often incredibly blunt about someone's career or situation. Nevertheless, his love of dance and dancers is endless and fiercely loyal.

In the beginning, when Misha took over, some people started to have difficulties in the company. When he started to use other dancers, some of the dancers who were used to a lot of work weren't given much to dance. Naturally there was anger, and some people became hostile, furious even, and blamed Misha for their careers not getting anywhere. Unfortunately, it was the truth. As the director of the company, Misha has that power. But that's part of the director's job, sad as it is, in any company. I was fortunate to have benefited from the situation, but I could understand the confusion and frustration of the dancers who didn't. One of my close friends was one of them.

When I joined ABT, Gregory Osborne had been in the company for about two years. We became friends and, because we had similar looks, builds and coloring, were considered the "Bobbsey Twins" of American Ballet Theatre. At the time, Gregory was getting a lot to do because Glen Tetley the internationally-acclaimed, American-born choreographer, had staged several of his contemporary ballets for Ballet Theatre (*Sacre du Printemps, Sphinx, Gemini,* and *Voluntaries*), and Glen liked Gregory's dancing. For the 1978-79 Season, Tetley was staging his ballet *Pierrot Lunaire* (in which Gregory later danced the title role) and a new work, *Contredances,* for Natalia Makarova and Anthony Dowell. Gregory and I were the two male soloists. Putting the two of us together in *Contredances* made us look like bookends.

The music by Anton Webern was very difficult and I was adamant about getting everything correct and on the music. I was 19 years old and, being young, didn't think that wanting everything to be perfect was too much to ask. I tried very hard to make it that way. I began to sense a feeling of resentment or competition from Gregory, and I had a difficult time. During a rehearsal before the premiere of *Contredances* in Chicago, we still weren't together. I thought Gregory was acting rather flip. He wasn't focusing and we weren't getting anywhere. He was pissing me off and I started to tell him so. Scott Douglas, the ballet master, got furious and threatened to take me out of the ballet. He didn't understand that I simply wanted to get everyone dancing together. At the same time, Peter Fonseca was trying to do the same thing in the corps de ballet. Being very musical, Peter could figure out any kind of counts to any kind of music.

Scott Douglas asked me to have a drink and talk over what was going on in rehearsals. When we met for drinks, I told him, "I don't think we really know what we're doing when we rehearse this ballet. People aren't concentrating." He agreed, but he told me to worry only about what *I* had to do and not worry about anyone else. "Okay, fine," I said. The important lesson here was to take care of my own business and leave the rehearsing to the balletmaster. My friendship with Gregory continued unscathed.

When Misha took over ABT, it was obvious that he liked my dancing. After *Prodigal Son,* he began to cast me in one soloist and principal role after another. I woke up one day and thought, "I'm doing all of these wonderful ballets, but what about my friend Gregory?" Misha just wasn't casting him in things, whereas under Lucia he was dancing all the time. With Misha, things completely turned around. He didn't like certain dancers in certain ballets, and Gregory was one of them.

I felt Gregory and I were equally as talented. He didn't have the biggest jump and his pirouettes weren't always the best, but he had better line and feet than I did. Certain aspects of his physicality were better-suited to ballet than mine. But it was just a personal thing with Misha.

It's hard to say exactly why a director cares more for one dancer than another, but I think it boils down to being a matter of someone's personal taste. It made me realize how much our artistic lives are in other people's hands. In the beginning, I was in a situation where Lucia didn't even know my name. (She sometimes called me Richard Schafer and I never bothered to correct her.) That's why I wanted to leave Ballet Theatre. I didn't think I had a future. Now Gregory knew how I had felt.

Gregory and I dealt with the situation the best we could as two young adults. When I became friendly with Charles France, my friendship with Gregory never lessened, but I didn't spend as much time with him, Peter, and my other friends. This coincided with the turn in Gregory's situation and he might have thought that I didn't care about him as a friend anymore, which wasn't the case at all. I was trying to live up to the trust that Misha had placed in my artistic development and focused primarily on my repertoire which continued to expand. I was cast for the leads in *Cinderella, Follow the Feet, Wild Boy,* and *La Sylphide.*

Erik Bruhn, the great Danish premier danseur, came back to ABT to teach us *La Sylphide.* He brought everything he had ever learned about being on the stage into the rehearsal room. He could help a dancer in the most productive way by being positive about the individual he was working with. His teaching and coaching were very personal, and you never doubted he was working with *you,* not with "just another dancer." Erik never passed judgment in the rehearsal room. You always felt that he liked you as a dancer.

Erik appreciated Gregory's dancing and wanted him to learn James, the leading male role in *La Sylphide,* but Gregory wasn't one of the first four casts. He was crushed and soon after told me that he was thinking about leaving Ballet Theatre. It was clearly a decision no one could make for him, but I advised him to think very seriously about it. I felt that if he held out, eventually Misha would need him and things would work out. But I told him if he was really unhappy with his situation, he should leave. He did. Erik Bruhn succeeded Alexander Grant as Artistic Director of the National Ballet Of Canada in 1984, and Gregory accepted his invitation to join as principal dancer.

Gregory Osborne was a soloist before I was. I was promoted to soloist in the Spring of 1981, then principal dancer in 1983, and Gregory remained a soloist. Seeing a friend surpass you is hard for someone to deal with, but I think Gregory handled it well. We never fought. He was always supportive and happy for me. But it must have taken its toll inside, I'm sure. This situation is inherent in dancers' friendships. We're happy for a friend's success but, "What about me?" Gregory always respected that part of our friendship. He never allowed his ego to get in the way of my progress. He respected my success.

Usually in cases where dancers needed to vent their frustrations, instead of going to Misha, who was often busy rehearsing productions and dancing himself, they went to Charles with their problems. Charles was the sounding board for the dancers, the intermediary between them and Misha. As the years went on, many people found it difficult to separate what was Misha and what was Charles. They didn't recognize that what Charles did was always Misha's decision.

At one point in 1981, the rumors got very bad. Elaine Kudo, Charles and I decided we wanted to stay at the Grove Isle Club, a first-class hotel in Miami, rather than in the usual Holiday Inn. So we did just that. Elaine and I rented a car and Charles had his own car. It happened that Misha stayed in the same hotel, which belonged to friends of his. Of course they always gave Misha first-class treatment, including an Alfa Romeo for his use.

I heard later through the grapevine at David Howard's studio in New York that Elaine and I had stayed in a deluxe hotel, with a chauffeured limousine paid for by American Ballet Theatre. It was a joke. Rumors like that are so absurd there's little that can be done about them. It certainly doesn't help to honor them by getting defensive. We knew the truth and didn't have to defend ourselves.

But, sadly, people don't often want to know the truth. They want life to be like a soap opera. Soap operas on television can be great escapes from reality, where you can believe in the extremes and absurdities of life. But people were turning my situation in the company into a soap opera. At one point it got back to me that I was sleeping with Charles *and* Misha. Basically, the rumors were more harmful for Misha than anyone else. I could overlook much of it, since I knew my career advanced because Misha liked my dancing. But Misha's reputation and his career as a director were at stake when things like that were said. Later, when the actress Jessica Lange and Misha broke up, he started dating Lisa Rinehart, a girl in the company. Lisa was in the corps de ballet and did a few solos. When she began her relationship with Misha, it really had no effect on her career. That was not Misha's way. He didn't play favorites with people he liked or women he was attracted to. He put dancers out on stage for their dancing ability, regardless of whether or not they were offstage personalities he would like to spend time with. It was apparent in Gelsey's situation. They didn't have a very good relationship, but as long as he was able, he put her out on stage. That's the way a company should function. You can't have all your friends working for you. It doesn't work that way.

I can only say that if Misha ever leaves ABT, I certainly hope they can find someone as good, because he's a tough act to follow. After being away for a while, I can see objectively how he's changed the company in such a dramatic way, from the corps de ballet to principal dancers. He has refurbished the whole standard of dancing in ABT. The younger dancers who are dancing principal roles have progressed to high levels of artistic performance that are encouraging to American dance.

When Lucia was around, Alicia Alonso came to dance *Giselle,* and the company restaged the entire production for her. I was one of the peasants in the corps. We were split up into A, B and C groups, and what we had to do was calculated down to the last detail, especially the "Mad Scene." Due to her ongoing battle with blindness, Alonso was an extreme case, but every time a new guest artist came in, we had to do a slightly different version. It was such nonsense. The production lacked continuity it might have had, had we stuck to one concept. You can't continually turn a production around and expect it to have a consistent artistic vision.

Misha has had a few guest artists, but they are a rarity. Foreign artists are not really needed since the level in Europe is completely different than in America. When Jean-Charles Gil came to dance *Giselle*, for example, everything was stylistically so different that he looked out of place. It was out of context with the total concept of the *Giselle* ABT currently performs. Misha now insists that guest artists when he has them learn ABT's productions. Still, the varying dance and performance styles of some foreign artists often look odd or incongruous. There's really no worthwhile long-term effect for the company in anyone coming for one or two performances although it *is* an opportunity for audiences to appreciate foreign artists.

Lucia Chase focused on the box office and personalities, but the productions suffered. ABT's *Swan Lake* had been around for twenty years and *Giselle* had been around forever. Many of the costumes were so old with sweat that dancers had to douse them with perfume before putting them on. Misha made salaries more equitable and put money into new productions. If you're working in a company situation your goal is the good of the entire company, not the benefit of the individual. It was one of the many lessons I learned from ABT under Misha's directorship.

San Francisco was always my favorite city on tour. It was such a pleasure working there because it wasn't just work. You could spend free hours in fascinating antique shops and first-class restaurants, or on day trips in the beautiful Bay area. But work was a total pleasure, too, because we performed in their magnificent old War Memorial Opera House. ABT always appeared in San Francisco before Los Angeles, and I hated leaving there for "La La Land."

Misha had injured himself before the opening night of our 1981 season in Los Angeles. He was scheduled to dance with Natasha Makarova in Jerome Robbins' *Other Dances*, which I had learned and performed with Susan Jaffe.

I was asked to replace Misha, but this time it was with

Natalia Makarova, *the* Prima Ballerina. I felt confident that I would look no better than an amateur dancing with one of the world's great artists of the dance. But it was too big of a chance to turn down. In fact, it was one of the most exciting events of my career.

Natasha and I had one two-hour rehearsal the day of the performance. I expected a difficult time, but she was a dream. She was very tolerant of my partnering and never complained. I think she was a little tired and wanted to save her energy for that night. To conserve her strength, she "marked," basically walked through, the rehearsal. On the other hand, I, as usual, did it full out on nerves alone.

Through it all, ballet mistress Elena Tchernichova sat in front of the room and watched calmly with one leg tightly crossed and wrapped around the other, her "100s" cigarette suspended deftly from her fingers as if it were at the end of a silver cigarette holder *a la* pantherine silent movie star. An expert in demonstrating the classical Russian style of the Kirov school to the company in the full length classics, Elena was Natasha's frequent coach. I was happy to have her there as our "third eye" for *Other Dances,* Jerry Robbins' study in the richness of Russian character dance in a classical mode. Our two hours were up. I thanked Natasha and Elena, kissing each one in turn.

"Relax, *Rhaubby,*" Elena assured me in her "laid-back" voice, "Vill be vonderful, you know."

The rehearsal came late in the day, and I had to go straight to the theatre from the rehearsal studio of the Los Angeles Ballet. There was lots to do from makeup and warm-up barre to spraying my shoes. Charles picked me up at the studios and as we drove along the freeway to the theatre, we talked about the performance that night. I think Charles was as excited as I was. Suddenly, out of the blue came this huge Goodyear blimp slowly floating in the sky overhead.

Remembering all the Russian superstitions Natasha believes in—never mix red and white flowers (death), don't put pointe shoes on the dressing table—I thought quickly.

"Did you know that it's good luck to drive under a blimp?" I said with total conviction to Charles.

"No!" he said in amazement.

"Absolutely," I continued. "It's something I heard about in Texas." Charles loves good luck symbols and chose to believe me.

Later at the theatre, I was so nervous putting on my makeup that my eyelids looked like a road map. Beads of sweat ran from the bridge of my nose, melting the pancake. I resigned myself to a less than perfect makeup job, thinking there were more important things to concentrate on, like pulling some technique out of my hat! I did a quick warm-up. I was in a state of panic. Was this all a dream? Was I in super slow motion, never quite catching up with the time? I just wasn't *ready*!

Charles tried to calm me down, but I stood backstage as if I were a state's witness about to be called to the stand. And the audience, thousands of eyes, were my jury. I was replacing *Misha*. They were not, I feared, getting what they paid for.

"Pull it together, La Fosse," I said to myself. "It's only a ballet."

Natasha was off preparing herself to give her usual star performance. I looked at her and thought, I'm sorry *now*, Natasha, for any mistakes I might make. Merde? Good luck? What should I say to her?

She came to me instead and said, "Vee have fun, Robby. You see!"

The curtain went up. The audience applauded the moment we went on—I *knew* it wasn't for me—but it felt good anyway. From start to finish, the performance went completely opposite from anything I expected.

I always noticed that Natasha had an unusual approach to

music and prepared myself to dance slower. It was nothing of the sort. I think it was the most musical experience of my life. Balanchine may choreograph music, but Natasha can *dance* it. As they say in the song, "I could have danced all night!"

After the performance Charles came backstage and said, "It was great; you and Natasha looked wonderful together. That blimp must have really worked for you!"

"Oh, Charles," I said with a laugh, "I just made that one up!"

"You've got to be kidding!" he said, raising an eyebrow.

"Well"—I shrugged—"someone has to start superstitions, just like rumors!"

The following spring season, I made my debut at the Met as Albrecht in *Giselle* with Cynthia Harvey as my Giselle. Over the years, Misha had personally coached me in every leading role in this ballet, from the *Peasant Pas de Deux* to Hilarion to Albrecht. One of the greatest gifts I received from Misha was the enormous amount of time he spent with me on *Giselle*, going through the ballet with me every inch of the way, fine-tuning my character and technique in each role; sharing with me his knowledge of the tradition of classical mime acquired through his training in Russia. I don't think I was ever more prepared for a ballet in my career than I was for *Giselle*.

Nevertheless, it always helps to receive "merdes," the ballet world's word for good luck gifts from friends. Two hours before the performance, I walked into my dressing room to prepare and there, suspended from the ceiling, was a miniature Goodyear blimp with a kiddie tricycle under it, ready for a rider. It was Charles's "merde" to me. My debut went very well and I was sure that in some way, Charles's blimp brought me good luck. Charles had a way of keeping a good "tradition" alive!

John McFall, a choreographer from the San Francisco Ballet, was scheduled to create a ballet for Misha for the 1982-83 season. I was called to the rehearsal. I expected the usual, a story ballet with Misha as a man and me, alter ego, or something of the sort. In any case, it was exciting to be called to a rehearsal alone with Baryshnikov.

When we got into the rehearsal room, it was obvious that this ballet wasn't at all what I had imagined. First of all, the music was Stravinsky's "Ebony Concerto," a popular favorite with choreographers because of its jazzy, syncopated rhythms. It wasn't a story ballet at all. It simply was going to be two guys just dancin' and jumpin' around.

The ballet, called *Follow the Feet,* opened with Misha alone onstage. He did some stylized movements and covered the stage in a way that only he can do!

Then, from nowhere, I came on doing an aerial—a cartwheel with no hands—one of my most difficult acrobatic tricks, trying to steal the scene from Misha. The ballet turned out to be a sort of "Anything you can do, I can do better" in dance. It's no mystery who did better. I wasn't sure if the ballet would work, but it was worth the try.

Misha was always completely absorbed in the rehearsals. He gave 100 percent and was always professional. He never brought his outside concerns or problems into the room. He was easy to work with, and we never had anything even resembling a fight. Does it sound kind of boring? It wasn't at all. It was truly exciting working with such a total professional. It was just one example of why he is the great artist he is.

The ballet was filled with tricky lifts. One that I particularly liked became very popular with audiences. Misha ran towards me, stuck his foot in the palms of my clenched hands and using them as a springboard, bounced off, high into the air.

At one point, John McFall wanted me to lift Misha over my head. I was game for anything. But Misha was a little apprehensive. He didn't want me to injure myself. That first time, I failed, and Misha wanted to end it right there. I insisted we try it again. I was determined to lift a superstar over my head! The second time, I still had trouble. Seeing their questioning looks, I asked for one more chance. "Please, just one more time. Come on, Misha. I know I can do it. Third time's the charm!" I said with a little laugh. I did it.

Audiences loved *Follow the Feet*, but the critics weren't particularly crazy about it. Thank God, they at least seemed to enjoy Misha and me just "struttin' our stuff." They never said I didn't deserve to dance opposite Misha, which I found not only a relief, but flattering. In fact, it was in this ballet that I was referred to for the first time as Baryshnikov's protege.

Chapter 11

IN the fall of 1983, ABT was precariously in the red. The loss of touring revenues resulting from a long dancer's strike begun in September, 1982, and not settled until late that year was said to be a major contributing factor. Rumors were that the company might fold, and a miracle, most likely in the form of a major new production, was needed. The much-needed "miracle" had actually been started before the strike, in late summer 1982. It was Prokofiev's full-length *Cinderella*, with choreography by Mikhail Baryshnikov and Peter Anastos, former member and founder of Les Ballets Trocadero de Monte Carlo, the famous travestie ballet company.

Prokofiev's score had always been one of my favorites, ever since I saw Edmund in Ben Stevenson's beautiful production for the National Ballet of Washington. The music has wit, mystery and romance, just like the fairy tale itself. Rehearsals resumed in the fall of 1983, and I was called to rehearsals to learn the Prince, with Lise Houlton as my Cinderella.

But . . . I was also learning one of the Ugly Stepsisters. I had played a biblical figure, sailors, cowboys, outlaws, poets, aristocrats and assorted anonymous/abstract roles, but *never* a woman. From the beginning I didn't approach the role as a simple case of putting on a costume, a wig and pointe shoes. I considered it a matter of transformation.

I began with research, which is how I always approached a new role, but it wouldn't be through photographs, films, books or history this time. I was going to look around and observe the traits and characteristics of women around me. I took note of the way they walked, the way they talked (isn't that a song?), the way they moved, the way they held themselves.

Hands and neck were the two things I noticed that were most different between men and women. Well, maybe not the *only* two. Men look at their fingernails, for example, with palms facing them and fingers bent, while women observe nails with fingers straight and the backs of their hands facing them. Men's necks tend to be set on their heads at slight angles, while women hold their necks, which are usually longer and thinner, more upright. I didn't plan plastic surgery for my neck, but I knew I could alter another feature. I could raise my eyebrows. Women seem to have higher eyebrows and longer lashes than men. False eyelashes, by the way, are a *bitch* to put on. Why do some women *do* it?

Of course, Peter Anastos was a natural at demonstrating what he wanted from the parts, but Victor Barbee (the other Ugly Sister) and I had some trouble making the parts our own. For a while we kept coming up with the same characters. But Peter kept working with us, wanting one to be dumb and ditzy and the other a conniving bitch. Naturally, I got "dumb and ditzy" (what do they always say about blonds?). In the end, I think I came off more as a nervous twit.

At one pointe Misha thought it advisable to start an "Ugly Stepsisters" pointe class, taught by Georgina Parkinson. Victor Barbee, Johan Renvall, Brian Adams, Michael Owen, Peter Fonseca, David Cuevas and myself, the men from the different casts came into the room, sat down, slipped on our toe shoes, tied our ribbons, and stood at the barre waiting for Georgina. From the start, it was pretty hard to keep a straight face, but we did our best. Despite her Royal Ballet ballerina bearing, Georgina has an incredible sense of humor and appreciation of the absurd. She walked into the room, looked around and envisioning what would follow said, *"This* is going to be a real *camp!"* From the outset, it was a three-ring circus. We were in hysterics. I showed her my best hops on pointe with a *petite ronde de jambe* a la *Giselle*; Victor Barbee did thrilling releves in grand diva manner; Johan Renvall whipped off thirty-two *fouettes,* like the virtuoso he is. Laughing out loud, Georgina threw her head back and screeched in her proper British accent, "This is *fahr*-fucking-out!"

Those classes *were* pretty "far-fucking-out," but they did *wonders* for our technique!

It was during the process of putting together *Cinderella* that my urge to choreograph became obvious to me. The bottom line is, the ballet just wasn't coming together. Throughout rehearsals, I would make suggestions. Peter and Misha rejected most of them. Can you imagine?! They wanted it to be their own. Now, having choreographed several pieces, I understand why.

Somehow the production got assembled, with elaborate sets and beautiful costumes by Santo Loquasto. Visually, it looked like a surefire hit. The choreography was still unfocused. And the choreography wasn't alone. Throughout all the usual stage rehearsals in Washington, I kept changing my makeup and character. It still wasn't where I wanted it to be.

The day of the premiere, I woke up with a fever but thought nothing of it. I went to Kennedy Center and started my daily routine, just like any woman of the theatre. But my fever didn't go down. At one point, I looked down at my arm and noticed little red spots, a kind of rash. I had no idea what was happening. I thought it might be an allergic reaction to something I ate. I went to show Charles. "CHICKEN POX!" he shrieked. He immediately got on the phone and called the doctor.

As he dialed, I said, "But Charles, I thought only children

got chicken pox!" As I spoke, I tried to remember having them as a child and couldn't.

I went to the doctor and Charles' diagnosis was correct. Soon after I got back to my hotel room, Charles called me. He told me Deirdre Carberry, a young soloist, had called not five minutes earlier to tell him she had come down with chicken pox! We could only laugh.

"I don't know if anyone knows your part well enough to go on for you," Charles said.

"Don't worry about it," I said, "I want to do my performance chicken pox or no!"

So there I stood, five minutes before curtain, in total drag and a fever of 105 degrees! But, if I say so myself, I was still the most beautiful—and the *hottest* (yes, pun intended)—Ugly Stepsister you'd ever seen. Singing high C's as I strapped on my pointe shoes, I was now covered with red spots!

Chicken pox was not the only physical ailment to afflict dancers in *Cinderella.* The day after the first dress rehearsal, the blisters on my heels were so swollen I couldn't get my pointe shoes on. I danced the whole day with my heels out of my shoes. By the third day, I knew firsthand the pain ballerinas complain about. OUCH!!

"I don't know if I can *take* this much longer," moaned Michael Owen, one of the Sisters in another cast. "Maybe I shouldn't *do* this part. I enjoy being a *man!*"

There's no question that enduring the pain of putting on pointe shoes on a daily basis is definitely masochistic. Thank God I didn't have to make a career of it.

As it turned out, the pain was worth it. *Cinderella* was a huge success with the public, not only at its premiere in Washington, (after which I succumbed and was laid up for a week with those little red spots) but throughout our national tour. The critics, however, *hated* it! Nevertheless, it was sold out for nearly every performance and made the company a greal deal of money. ABT would be back on the boards for at least another season or two.

Misha hasn't choreographed since then.

Rumor and controversy seemed to be the rule at ABT throughout 1983-84. Sources from within and outside the company were, in many cases, questioning the wisdom of Misha's directorship. The company seemed to be adrift in a flood of negative press and public opinion. Many dancers felt that the money spent on new productions could be better spent on dancers' salaries. Misha was under fire from the board of directors, who wanted him to hire guest artists to increase box office receipts. Everyone was trying to tell Misha what to do. He must have felt like he was between a rock and a hard place, and he went through a period where he thought he might give it all up and quit the company. At one point, I remember him saying, "Maybe I'll just leave with a small group of dancers, and we'll go to Monte Carlo and start a company there." I had heard that under similar circumstances, George Balanchine had said the same thing several years before. I said, "Fine. I'll go. I'm ready."

Another ongoing controversy concerned Misha going off and doing films and television specials and not being around the company enough for three months out of the year. There were bad repercussions in the press. Rumor had it that Misha wasn't really running the company—Charles France was. It was getting to be an ugly mess.

The facts were that while Misha was away, he had *all* his assistants and ballet masters taking care of the situation, and they did a very fine job. Of course, when Misha *was* around, it was always better. He devoted so much time to the dancers in rehearsal, and his presence was so powerful, that he could pull together in an hour what another ballet master would take two or three rehearsals to accomplish. He knew exactly how to tell the dancers what to do technically and stylistically. He worked especially hard and well with the corps de ballet. Of course with Misha, the dancers were more alert and well behaved.

But the pressures didn't affect Misha alone, there were repercussions throughout the company, even in the "highest places." Executive Director Herman Krawitz resigned and Donald M. Kendall, Chairman of the Board, left soon after.

Understandably, Misha was fed up during that period and considered leaving the company. He had limitless options. He could do anything he chose. He could make a fortune on dancing alone. We didn't know at the time that someday he would have his own line of dancewear, a perfume, or whatever. And there was always Monte Carlo.

So, after ABT got back from a summer engagement in Philadelphia, Misha planned to get away and think things over. He wanted to be near the beach, yet close enough to the city in case he needed to be there in a hurry for emergency meetings or whatever. He chose a house on the ocean side of Fire Island and went out there with Lisa Rinehart. A while later, he invited me and Charles and Susan Jones to come out and visit and we all went out for a week.

We didn't do much. We watched a lot of tennis. Martina Navratilova was in peak form but Hana Mandlikova was our favorite. We stayed up nights playing card games and Dictionary. We made nice dinners and took long walks. Misha went fishing on the ocean in the mornings and caught some fish. We played charades and listened to music—you know, your typical, fabulous Lifestyles-of-the-Rich-and-Famous activities. Misha didn't play very much. We listened to Karen Akers tapes and the original cast album of *La Cage aux Folles.* Our favorite song was "The Best of Times is Now," ironically enough, considering the situation at ABT.

Charles was very, very upset. He felt that it might be the end of his career at ABT. Having been Misha's associate for so many years, he felt that if Misha left ABT, he wouldn't stay on, and doubted that he would find work anywhere else in the ballet world that would mean as much. He frankly wouldn't have wanted to work with anyone else. Charles is really devoted to ABT. He didn't like this dissension and wanted Misha to stay on. It was very hard on him and he stayed in the house all the time, barely seeing the light of day.

For the entire week, I tried my hardest to make this week a vacation for everyone. One day, I got all of us drunk on fruit daiquiris. *La Cage* was playing and we were carrying on in the pool. Susan Jones was feeling pretty good. She jumped into the pool and was laughing so hard that she upchucked a volcano of fruit daiquiris. She didn't miss a beat. She kept right on having a good time. She got out of the pool, still laughing. We were trying very hard to have a laid-back, relaxing time. But it was very difficult. Personally, I didn't know what the right thing to do was in this situation. I was especially worried and concerned for Charles.

Kenneth came out for the weekend with this very bizarre tape he had made especially for the occasion. It had everything from Nancy Sinatra singing "These Boots Were Made for Walkin'" to songs from old musicals and movies, sixties rock-and-roll and contemporary music by Laurie Anderson. We loved it, but Misha really hated it because it was loud. He wanted to listen to Willie Nelson, but we didn't have any.

The night of the Miss America Pageant we gave a party and invited a group of friends who were out on the Island. I made banners for everyone to wear—they read "Miss Conduct," "Miss Behave," "Miss Take," "Miss Givings," "Miss Demeanor" and so on, in keeping with an irreverent evening. It was the year Vanessa Williams won. I liked the first runner-up, the girl who eventually replaced her, because she was a better singer. Everyone else liked Vanessa because she was prettier. Actually I didn't care who won, I just thought it would be exciting for a black girl to win.

Anyway, our party was a disaster. Peter Fonseca came, but no one else bothered to show up. We were all pretty poor company; it was just one of those evenings when no one felt like "hanging out." We all wanted to go to bed, so we called it a night pretty early.

I had trouble sleeping and about one in the morning gave in to the urge to go out for the night air and maybe take in a few dances at the Pavillion, a popular disco on Fire Island. I hadn't danced a step in almost a week. I got up, dressed and sneaked out of the house without anyone hearing me, and went directly to the disco.

The place was packed with steamy bodies writhing to blaring disco music left over from the late seventies. Since I didn't really like disco much anymore, it didn't make me feel like dancing. Instead I stood to one side looking for people I knew, and didn't see anyone. All of a sudden, there across the dance floor, appeared this face, almost out of nowhere. It was a very strong face, one I thought maybe I recognized. He was just staring at me. I stared back. We worked our way slowly toward each other and introduced ourselves. His name was Steven. He asked me to dance, but I still didn't feel like dancing. I did offer to go outside and talk.

Steven told me he was originally from St. Louis, was a Harvard graduate, now a singer, and that he worked out. He had a short military-type haircut. Given his appearance, it was slightly incongruous that he had a rather high tenor voice. I later learned he could change the pitch of his voice at will, from high to deep, especially when singing.

In the course of the conversation, he told me he had worked at a restaurant called Star Thrower Café. It was then that I realized I had seen him before when Kenneth and I used to go to Star Thrower all the time when Kenneth first came to New York. It was a small, inexpensive restaurant down in the Village, with very good food. I remembered Steven as being much thinner, but I remembered him, which

146

was the important thing. He knew that I was a dancer. The idle chat continued and he told me he had recently come into some money and wasn't currently working. He was using the time to make some studio recordings.

He asked me to dance again. This time I agreed. It wasn't worth it. It was obvious Steven didn't like making a public display of himself on the dance floor, and I didn't want him to either. I knew by then that there was something I wanted and it wasn't the next dance. We left the dance floor and kept on going. He invited me over to where he was staying and I accepted. A warm breeze was blowing as we walked side by side along the boardwalk through the trees. My whole body tingled with the sense that something very exciting was about to happen.

Steven was staying in a small house on the bay side, surrounded by trees. Once inside, we opened a bottle of red wine. It had been chilled, which was something new to me. He lit some candles and what followed was one of the most passionate experiences of my life. It was simply extraordinary. There seemed to be no limit to the feelings we needed to express to each other. We had no control over it. It seemed right and inevitable.

Later, I felt I had to explain my situation to Steven. I told him I would be on the Island only until the end of the week. He was staying for another two. The house was very small, with an outdoor shower and a bedroom that barely accommodated a full bed. But life on Fire Island is not about how big your house is. For one thing, you spend most of your time on the beach. I explained that being Misha's guest, I couldn't invite someone I had just met to the house. Luckily, he understood.

The next day I didn't see Steven, but I couldn't stop thinking about him. I even thought about him that night as I stood in the kitchen washing lettuce for salad. The whole side of Misha's house facing the beach, including the kitchen, had floor-to-ceiling windows. Turning around to make the salad, I glanced through the glass and had the strangest feeling that someone was watching me from the beach in the darkness. I couldn't see anyone, so shrugged it off and went on making dinner.

Two days later, I met Steven on the beach. It was like meeting him for the first time all over again. I was so intrigued, I wanted to be with him every minute. Feeling that way about someone makes you very nervous. You want to say and do the right thing, but you also want to be yourself. Of course on the beach, wearing only a bathing suit, it's fairly difficult not to be yourself, at least your physical self. During our talk, Steven told me that he had gone out the night before for a walk on the beach and, passing our house, stopped and watched me for almost an hour. Remembering that moment in the kitchen, I thought, "This guy gives off some powerful vibrations!"

We saw each other a few more times, but at the end of the week I had to go back to the city and start working. After that week I returned to New York knowing that this wasn't going to be just one of those summer things. We would definitely be seeing each other in the city. After years of avoiding the possibility of any long-term relationships, considering "love" of secondary importance to my career, I felt Steven breaking down every last shred of resistance. From that point on, in fact, I can't remember a day going by without speaking to him on the phone or seeing him. When he got back to the city, I went to spend the night and simply never stopped. Little by little, I started leaving my clothes there. Conveniently, he lived downtown on Tenth Street, much closer than my apartment on the Upper West Side to the ABT studios on Nineteenth Street.

Living with Steven was not only about passion. It was also about fun. We enjoyed doing the most simple things together. Before the rehearsal period started, we spent a weekend at

Niagara Falls for a kind of mock honeymoon. We stayed in a hotel overlooking the Falls. There was a typical tourist-trap amusement park that was great fun. We laughed a lot. Our being together was what mattered. We learned a lot about mutual consideration. I was allergic to his two cats and woke up one night unable to breathe. Steven went out at four in the morning to an all-night drug store to get me an antihistamine. What else could he do? For a while he tried locking the cats in the bathroom, but it was useless. The hair was everywhere. The first three months of our relationship, we stayed home a lot, getting to know each other.

Chapter 12

STEVEN'S important addition to my life coincided with my work on Kenneth MacMillan's *Romeo and Juliet*.

The moment I heard that *Romeo and Juliet* was coming into the repertoire of ABT, I was very excited, feeling that Romeo was a role I was well suited to and whose story I understood. I planned to do a lot of research by studying videotapes of the ballet and to contact Georgina Parkinson, who would be teaching the leading roles. During our layoff, I called Georgina and asked her if she would go over the balcony pas de deux and variation with me in case I was called to learn Romeo. Leslie Browne had danced the balcony pas de deux with Misha in the movie *The Turning Point*, so I asked her to help too. They both agreed.

Leslie Browne and I went into the rehearsal room, about two weeks before rehearsals were supposed to start, and worked on the pas de deux. I wanted so much to be prepared that it was worth renting rehearsal space with my own money. Being out of shape, Leslie and I found it very hard work. It was slow going.

When Kenneth MacMillan created *Romeo and Juliet* for the Royal Ballet in 1965, the role of Juliet was made on his protegée Lynn Seymour, who had an extraordinary arabesque and whose body formed incredible curved, supple lines. Leslie

151

wasn't that kind of dancer, so we worked on lots of bending and stretching to achieve the choreography's specific look.

By the time the rehearsal period began I was so into my relationship with Steven that the passion called for in *Romeo and Juliet* was bubbling to the surface. I knew what Romeo must have felt for Juliet, wanting someone he couldn't have publicly, having a love he had to hide but unable to stop himself. Of course in Romeo's case, he wasn't in love with another guy. It wasn't Romeo and . . . Steven.

Of course my friends knew about Steven, and I wasn't concerned about most people in the ballet world, since most of them accept gay relationships. Nobody openly calls you a faggot. But my career was at a high point and I was becoming more publicly recognizable. I always had to consider what might get around to the outside world about my personal life. But that's what it was—my personal life. It had nothing to do with my public life and I intended to keep it that way.

In any case, *Romeo and Juliet* was just about the best thing I could have been working on at the time. Rehearsals began, and Marianna Tcherkassky started learning the ballet with Fernando, Susan Jaffe with Patrick Bissell, Amanda McKerrow with Kevin McKenzie and, surprisingly enough, Leslie and I were put together. When we started the rehearsal period, I was surprised to find there was a lot of jealousy concerning the fact that Leslie and I were already so prepared. I think some dancers suspected a conspiracy—that since Leslie and I had worked on *Romeo and Juliet* in advance, they weren't being given a fair chance. I felt caught in a situation of my own making. Yet I couldn't feel guilty about using my own time on my own layoff to get a little bit of an edge. Ballet is not a business where you say, "Please surpass me." I didn't get paid for all that work and had, in fact, paid for the rehearsal space. Anyone was free to have done the same.

I offered to use what I had learned to help others during rehearsals, and some accepted my help. But when Leslie and I weren't around, I suspect people talked about who, they assumed, would obviously be first cast. The thought of being first cast was not the primary thought in my mind. I simply wanted to ensure my chances of dancing a ballet I felt I truly understood and could really do. It had all the right elements to suit me: It wasn't 100-percent classical. It was romantic. I was young. I felt *Romeo and Juliet* was the ballet that could really make my career. What dancer given the chance wouldn't?

I worked very hard during rehearsals. The other Romeos were more experienced dancers and I needed to be more prepared. I was hoping that having had the extra two weeks would make the difference for me. Leslie, making a comeback, was in a similar situation. Her career had been in a slump, and Juliet could be the much-needed showcase for her talents. Sensing tension in rehearsals, Georgina stopped using us to demonstrate after a while. Taking Georgina's lead, we started to dance with other partners in rehearsal. This made sense, since final casting hadn't gone up. Kenneth MacMillan might come in and, at the last minute, decide he wanted Marianna and me together, or whatever.

Meanwhile, I did my homework. I went uptown and saw a very bad production of *Romeo and Juliet*. I read and reread the play and made a very important realization. As much as I might know the play from reading it, seeing it, and hearing the words, we were doing a *ballet*. There would be many elements of the play missing from the ballet. By the same token, many things given passing mention in the play would receive richer treatment in the ballet. Rosaline, for example, is only spoken of in the play, yet the first scene of the ballet centers on her flirtation with Romeo. The youthful abandon of Romeo and his friends, given free rein in their dance with the whores in the ballet, would be difficult even for Shakespeare to convey in the same way.

Another case in point is the fight between Mercutio and

Tybalt, where Romeo comes between them. It's a very hard thing to convey on stage and MacMillan chose not to do it. In the ballet, Mercutio more or less backs up into Tybalt's sword. So, early on, I just stopped trying to retain every detail from the play. You could drive yourself crazy.

I realized it was most important to concentrate on the *choreographer's* point of view. In his version of the ballet, Mac-Millan saw Juliet as the predominant character. It's *her* story rather than Romeo's that the viewer is made to follow. I always felt it was a struggle for all of the Romeos to make their character as prominent as Juliet's. Her almost overnight transformation from young girlhood to womanhood, through passion, overshadows Romeo's struggle with *his* passions, not only his passion for Juliet, but his passion to revenge the death of his friend Mercutio as well.

I understood Romeo's passion. Passion was the basis of my relationship with Steven. It didn't start gradually as a friendship. It was pure magnetism.

Living off investments, Steven was out of work at the time and devoted a lot of time to our relationship. His schedule basically fit around mine. When he wasn't with me, he spent most of his time at the library, researching scientific facts about vitamins for a computer software nutrition program and service he and a friend, Dr. Barry Gingell, planned to start. After a blood analysis, clients would be advised of vitamin deficiencies and how they could be corrected. I wasn't exempt.

Steven immediately encouraged me to start a rigorous vitamin and nutrition program. I ate kale, lots of green vegetables, all your basic healthful foods. I cut down on coffee and sugar. I also started taking arginine and ornithine, amino acids that augment muscle development and strength. The timing couldn't have been better. I needed as much strength as possible to get through *Romeo and Juliet.* I think this ballet requires more stamina than any ballet I know.

The first act alone is exhausting. After he dances with the whores in the first scene, a variation, a pas de trois and a short pas de deux with Juliet in the ballroom scene, Romeo dances the long balcony pas de deux including another variation. In Act II, there's a quick, demanding dance with a series of double saut-de-basques across the stage, followed by a short breather to marry Juliet. The big sword fight with Tybalt that follows is difficult to get through because it requires a great deal of anger, always a draining emotion. At this point you really have nothing left.

The ballet is a grueling experience, demanding the gamut of your emotions and enormous stamina. By the beginning of the third act, your calves and arches are so cramped, you question your ability to jump or even point your foot. Actually, the two pas de deux in the third act are not as physically demanding. The feeling of exhaustion even helps achieve the right mood for the bedroom pas de deux that opens the act. Lying there in bed before the curtain goes up, you really would like to just lie there with Juliet until the next morning. By the crypt scene, you're so drained it requires little motivation to welcome eternal rest.

In any case, the vitamins helped a lot. I stopped eating red meat and stuck with fish and poultry. I must have had a turkey sandwich for lunch every day for months. I drastically cut down my caffeine intake and switched to mineral water. Maintaining a healthy routine became a major factor in my life. McDonald's had never been a way of life with me, but I was now much more aware of what was good for me. Nutrition had never been one of my major concerns and I doubt I could have done it on my own. Doing it with Steven made it easy. When I spend a great deal of time with someone, I often take on many of their appealing characteristics and habits to bring us closer.

Physical demands aside, it was an easy rehearsal period for me because I was so excited about dancing *Romeo*. Toward the end of the rehearsal period, Kenneth MacMillan came to watch the different couples dance. At one point he called Leslie and me into his office and told us he wanted us to dance the first performance in Washington. My immediate reaction was to think of how the other dancers would react. I would have been satisfied with any performance, so long as I danced it. I wasn't sure I wanted the responsibility of being first cast.

I had heard somewhere that back in the sixties MacMillan had been forced to cast Fonteyn and Nureyev in *Romeo* for its New York premiere with the Royal Ballet, rather than Lynn Seymour and Christopher Gable, the original cast, because Sol Hurok insisted on it to assure proceeds at the box office. I think he wanted to have his way this time and cast younger dancers.

From the beginning I knew that my first performance wouldn't be my greatest by a long shot. I also knew that the critics would be expecting the greatest. I could have told them to forget it. I should have written an open letter to that effect.

As the season drew near, we had full run-throughs of *Romeo*. Watching the other dancers, I noticed the differences in interpretation and found things to learn. The atmosphere was generally good with the right amount of healthy competition. But there was still too much concern about who was first cast. Despite the honor and thrill of being first cast, I would have felt better about everything had Leslie and I not had to work in the intimidating shadow of opening night. But there wasn't much choice. I couldn't very well say, "I'm sorry, Kenneth. I really don't want to dance opening night of your ballet." It just doesn't work that way.

After our first run-through of the balcony pas de deux, the dancers were very kind to Leslie and me. They applauded in the rehearsal room, which is usually not done. It's a response usually reserved only for what dancers truly approve of. Applause takes time from rehearsals where time is of the essence. But customary behavior or not, they applauded and it was encouraging to feel the support of our peers. It was obvious that Leslie was going to be very, very good in the ballet. I couldn't tell about myself, but I was fortunate to have who I felt was the strongest Juliet.

Romeo and Juliet opened our Washington season in early December 1984, two days after my twenty-fifth birthday. I flew my parents and Lana up from Beaumont to see it, but I didn't have much time to enjoy Washington with them. Understanding that I had work to do, they didn't mind and were excited just to be able to see the performance. Opening night was a black-tie gala and my parents were invited.

"Do I have to wear a tuxedo?" my father asked, balking.

"No, Dad," I laughed. "You're my father. You can wear anything you want." Of course my mother went out and bought new dresses for Lana and herself.

After my rehearsals, I went up to their room in the Watergate Hotel. Since it was two days before my birthday, they had presents for me. My mother gave me a brown pillow, which didn't look like anything special. But when you put your head on it, it vibrated! I loved it. How many mothers would ever think to give their son a massage pillow? I got towels and sheets, which I always ask for. In return, I had Christmas presents for them.

Steven came down from New York and met my parents for the first time. Although they knew I had been living with him, we never discussed who Steven really was in my life. When my parents met him, they were very cordial. I sensed great concern from my parents. They were determined to make me feel completely at ease and treated him with great respect. They knew Steven meant a great deal to me, and they allowed me that. They all got along and conversation flowed smoothly. There seemed to be no problem about our relationship. I detected a little nervousness in my mother, at first, because she wanted so much to do and to say the right things. They liked him very much, which wasn't surprising.

It's very hard to dislike such an intelligent, well-mannered, well-groomed person. He's very much the image of the ideal son—even if he happens to be gay.

Not once during their visit did I ever sit down with my parents and have a discussion about what my relationship with Steven involved. It was just there. It made me very happy that he was accepted; that *I* was accepted. I was deeply moved by seeing my parents put aside whatever social conditioning they had and enjoy a person for who and what he was. As a young boy, I had often wondered how my family would react if I wanted someday to marry a black girl. In Washington, my parents showed that, unlike the Montagues or the Capulets, who realize too late, they cared only if a relationship is good for me. I was never so convinced of the strength of my parents' love for me as I was on that trip.

The final run-through of *Romeo and Juliet* went very smoothly. I felt confident about everything except the floor cloth they had put down on the stage. Usually dancers perform on battleship gray linoleum laid over the stage. That surface and ballet shoes, with the help of rosin on the shoes, create an excellent friction for feeling the floor, yet isn't resistant to pirouettes and fluid movement. The cloth floor, painted to match the colors of the decor, wasn't stretched enough, creating difficulty for the girls on pointe, and the shifting of the cloth resisted shoes, slowing down our turns. But nothing could be done. It was part of the ballet we simply had to get used to, one of those problems dress, stage and technical rehearsals are designed to make us aware of or take care of. The company morale was good. There were no arguments or complications.

Then came the performance, the most difficult of my life. It seemed the stars were not in my favor. I was nervous and on edge. Worried about the cloth floor, I treaded lightly. The constant struggle to get a sense of the floor made me worry more than usual about forgetting the choreography, an especially real fear in a three-act ballet. After all that rehearsing, hard work and enthusiasm, I just didn't feel ready.

When the curtain went up, time just slipped away. Before I knew it, I was in the crypt swallowing the "poison"—an empty bottle of air—Leslie stabbed herself and the curtain fell. The response was incredible. I didn't know if the audience was simply reacting to the ballet or to our performances. The wild applause and bravos went on and on, reminding me of the kind of applause I've given after performances I've loved. The response surpassed even the one for my debut in *Prodigal Son*.

Hearing the applause, I felt confused, knowing in my heart that my performance just wasn't there yet. I still felt too insecure and underdeveloped, even though I had gotten what I wanted out of some scenes. In general, the end of the ballet from the bedroom scene on to the crypt went well. The beginning called for a lot of work. But for the moment, the applause did my heart good.

A reception followed the performance. Steven had looked after my family during the performance and later brought them to the party. I came to the party exhausted and on edge and proceeded to get drunk. I felt terribly confused by a rush of mixed emotions. I was extremely happy that Steven and my family were there and getting along so well, but I felt great fear about what the critics would say. I had a very unsettling premonition that it wouldn't be good. Over the years, I had learned to control my problem with criticism, and reviews had never been that important to me. But it was *very* important to me not to be criticized in a detrimental way in this ballet. I would have welcomed constructive criticism, that would at least acknowledge potential in my performance.

When they came out, the reviewers' comments were beyond my worst expectations.

They weren't just bad, they were hateful.

I had never received anything so brutal. The first stage of my response was to believe that I wasn't being criticized for what I actually did in that performance; I was being attacked for my youth and relative lack of experience. This was my denial stage. It was obvious that the critic didn't want me on stage that opening night. He felt that the older members of the company, the more experienced artists such as Kevin McKenzie or Fernando should have been out there. He said some horrifying things. It was physically painful to read such hatred for a performance. I had often wondered how performers dealt with devastating reviews. Now I knew.

When the reviews came out for Kevin McKenzie it was clear to me that older, more experienced dancers were preferred, and I saw it also as a not-so-subtle attack on Misha's policy of casting younger dancers in principal roles. That's what I felt. It was at least my excuse to justify the review and go on. Otherwise I probably would have quit dancing then and there.

The second stage was acceptance. A few days after the review, I was at dinner at the Intrigue restaurant with a large group of friends from the company and, preoccupied by my thoughts, stared into space. "This is not the way things were supposed to go. This isn't happening," I told myself over and over. I couldn't deal with it. Not wanting to make a scene in front of my friends, I tried to control myself. It just hurt so much. Dancers live and work on a day-to-day basis with physical pain, but nothing prepares you for the hurt inflicted by the printed word. Tears rolled down my cheeks and I had to leave the table.

Of course my family and friends comforted me, assuring me that critics rarely know what they are talking about, questioning if the critic saw the same performance they say they did. The usual. Steven was supportive and helped me through it. He didn't try to explain the critics. He only knew what he saw. His opinion was that I gave a very good first performance and it would, of course, get better. If he, my parents and Charles hadn't been there, I'm sure my state of mind would have been much worse. They made me think of things other than my career and myself.

After my initial shock in response to the Washington review came a second wave of fear. Was I about to embark on a national tour to face this kind of response over and over again in cities across America? I did my second performance nevertheless, and it was already better. A question familiar to all performers crossed my mind, "Why don't the critics review the *progress*?" I felt more than ever that I would have fared better had I given the third- or fourth-cast performance and been spared the pressures of opening night, traditionally expected to be the best.

Fortunately, Leslie was a success. Both critics and audience liked her a lot. But she was angry. She felt the reviews were cruel and unfair to me and was very supportive. MacMillan also reassured me, telling me to pay no attention. He was pleased and thought I did very well. Of course he gave me helpful corrections. My timing had to be better in certain scenes. The opening with Rosaline had to be stronger, more raw and sexual. I had approached it more as a flirtation. He wanted the unabashed lustfulness of youth. Being the very first scene, it is the hardest. There's not much dancing, but an essential part of Romeo's character must be established through this flirtation and his relationship with his friends Mercutio and Benvolio. The impression that the three were lifelong friends would come across through the familiarity and ease gained from repeated performances by the same dancers. I had learned that lesson in *Fancy Free*.

The time came for my parents to leave. They knew that I was very upset, but there was nothing they could really say. There was nothing anybody could say that would erase the newsprint from my memory. It would take time for the wound to heal.

The third stage was anger. It made me want to continue doing that role. It made me think about it more than ever. I watched everyone else's performances to see what worked and what didn't. Watching from the audience, I realized more strongly how much the entire ballet is set up for Juliet, which made Romeo's role harder. Romeo doesn't have enough scenes to develop his character on stage before his best scenes with Juliet. Her scenes help explain her character. Romeo goes from "playboy" to fervent lover with very little transition between. The challenge was never so plain to me.

As a result of this experience, I finally understood what an ABT opening night really means to the critics. The audience gets all dressed up, wanting to see Natalia Makarova and Mikhail Baryshnikov. They want some glamor and the critics seem to reinforce that. I understood Margot and Rudolf's success in the American premiere of *Romeo and Juliet.* They were the international ballet superstars of the period.

I never went for a superstar performance I knew I couldn't deliver. Principal dancer or not, I wasn't a big major star. My focus was on doing MacMillan's choreography the way he wanted it done, by projecting youth and freshness. The audience seemed pleased, but I think the critics wanted the kind of performance that, at my age, I never could have delivered and never would have *wanted* to deliver, to be honest.

Still, it's ultimately a question of the choreographer's decision. I didn't put myself out there on stage opening night, yet I was the one who got the criticism.

The reviews also compared MacMillan's *Romeo and Juliet* to John Cranko's, which had been performed by the Joffrey Ballet. The consensus was that the crowd scenes in Cranko's were better, but the production values—the scenery and costumes—and the choreography for the pas de deux in Kenneth's were preferred.

I personally felt there were parts of the Cranko version that were more developed. His is more an ensemble piece where all the characters are strong, but I think it lacks the passion, the eroticism and sexual tension of Kenneth's. Kenneth's is not only more sensual, it's prettier to look at. I think it conveys more of the style and feeling of Prokofiev's score. Above all, the MacMillan version is a showcase for the passion of Romeo and Juliet.

Leslie was such a great actress that I instinctively knew what to do by following her lead. When you're on stage with someone who can act without pretense or insecurity, it makes you relax and feel confident in yourself as an actor, freeing you to respond and react without inhibition. Leslie also felt confident in her relationship with me. More often than not, mutual respect creates an ideal working relationship on stage. Sometimes, of course, mutual dislike makes partners work beyond themselves and their personal feelings, and theatrical sparks fly onstage. But because she was so intense in the part, Leslie definitely brought my performance up several levels. She actually transformed herself on stage from a teenage girl to a woman, a formidable challenge for any actress or dancer.

Steven didn't come on tour, but I kept in touch with him by phone. We spoke nearly every night, or at least every other night. It was difficult to talk to him over the phone . . . not difficult, but what I really had to say had to be said in person.

From Washington, we went to Miami, where Fernando danced Romeo in the opening-night performance. It was the natural thing to do, since he's from there and he has lots of family, friends and fans. It was a very exciting evening. I felt better about the performance I would do there, because it followed an older, more experienced dancer. Knowing they had been satisfied with his interpretation, I felt I was in a better position for them to accept mine. The critic there was a woman, Laurie Horn, and she liked my Romeo. Reading her review diminished the pain a little more and the "end of the world" I feared in Washington drifted a little farther away. I danced a matinee and someone, Fernando I think, had can-

163

celled the next day's performance, and I was scheduled to replace him. I'd have two chances in a row to work on developing the role. Normally the schedule permits only one or two performances of a full-length ballet in a week, followed by a week of repertoire, then two weeks or so before your next chance to perform it. At times, development can be rather slow.

After my performance, I decided to do my laundry in the theatre. I was in a hurry to leave, have dinner and rest up for the next day's performance. My mind was racing with thoughts of how I could improve my performance. It was very hot and I went to open the window. In a hurry and distracted by my thoughts, I didn't notice the window opened by using a crank, which was missing. I pushed on the window with my left hand and it went right through the paper-thin glass.

I immediately jerked my hand back in a reflex action, and my wrist jammed on the jagged glass. I pulled my wrist off the glass and saw a big flap of skin had been torn loose. Blood gushed from the wound. I ran, calling for help. Corps girls who hadn't gone yet heard the glass break, came running and saw me holding my wrist up, pressing it together with my right hand. The girls told me to go to Peter Marshall, the physical therapist, who was still in the theatre. I ran downstairs to see him leaving a trail of blood. Marianna Tcherkassky was at my side all the way, assuring me that I was going to be all right. Pale and shaking I went to Peter and begged him to do something. Blood was running everywhere.

Peter immediately bandaged the wrist, got me into a car and rushed me to a hospital emergency room. By the time we got there, I was ready to pass out. A specialist was called in to check for lacerated arteries, tendons or ligaments. Repairing damaged tendons or ligaments would require major surgery. Luck was with me. Only the skin was cut, but it was serious enough to require thirteen stitches.

Once the situation was under control, I stopped worrying about bleeding to death and started wondering why this had to happen when I was so looking forward to a second chance at *Romeo*. I was told it would take two weeks before the stitches could be taken out and I could start back to work. There was nothing to do but wait. I considered staying in bed for the rest of the Miami season, but wanting to stay in shape as much as possible, I did a little bit of class without holding onto the barre.

A few days after this incident, those ever-present rumors caught up with me in Miami. Gary Lisz called me from Washington, where he was living at the time. He was frantic. "My God, Robby, what's going *on*?! How could you *do* such a thing?"

"What are you talking about," I asked, "How could I have done *what*?"

"Slit your wrists, of course!" he shouted. "The papers here carried an article saying you had slit your wrists in Miami!"

"Calm down, Gary," I laughed, "it was only one wrist and it was an accident. I was pretty upset in Washington, but not upset enough to go that far! I'm fine. Really." I told him the whole story and we were both laughing about it by the time we hung up.

It was while driving on our day off in Miami with Elaine Kudo, my roommate on tour, that we heard some beautiful music on the radio. It was *Harold in Italy* by Berlioz. I told Elaine it was perfect for a ballet I had in mind based on Nathaniel Hawthorne's novella *Rappaccini's Daughter*. I immediately went out and bought a tape of the music. Having heard only the second and third movements on the radio, I knew it would be perfect when I heard the rest. It had just the right feeling of Florentine Italy, and dance images began to take shape in my mind. Gary and our playwright friend Robert Lord had suggested the story to me, thinking it would

165

make a great ballet, and they were right. I found a new excitement in the idea of doing some choreography and decided to start work on the ballet while still on tour.

Throughout that tour, my performances in *Romeo and Juliet* improved as we went along. But it seemed most male critics had something similarly negative to say about my Romeo. Oddly enough, what the male critics disliked about my performance was what the female critics *liked*! What could I conclude but that, in essence, I appealed to women more than to men.

I learned a lot the year of *Romeo and Juliet*. It was a very hard year for me; a time of mixed emotions. I was having a certain amount of success; getting a lot of publicity because of my performances in *Romeo*; and an increased insight into partnering through my work with ABT's ballerinas. But I had a stressful time with the critics. They made me realize how much artists' lives are ruled by the written word.

The critical response to my debut in *Romeo and Juliet* stayed with me a long time. It was the most upsetting thing that ever happened to me professionally, because, although I never took well to criticism, I never realized that I valued it so much. One of the ways dancers try to overlook the written word, is to say that critics often don't know what they're talking about. That helps for a while, but the pain of seeing something negative in print about your life's work doesn't vanish easily. Through my experience with *Romeo and Juliet,* I finally realized that the pen was mightier than the sword.

Chapter 13

I didn't know I had a gift for partnering when I was a young dancer growing up. Schools didn't teach it. I partnered dancers in Marsha Woody's recitals, of course, but I never had lessons in actually how to do what I was asked to do. I just did it. The School of American Ballet offers pas de deux class, but they don't really teach you how to partner. They get you in a room and give combinations. But if you're doing a classical ballet or a modern ballet, it's much different than doing combinations. Partnering is something a dancer doesn't really really learn until he gets into a professional company.

A contributing factor to my ability to partner might come from the fact that as a kid I had a lot of experience on the stage. I suppose when you're young, your instincts for partnering are fresher. You attack the movement the way your body instinctively tells you to. Partnering has a lot to do with sensing how weight is balanced and counterbalanced. It's like playing tug of war. In tug of war, you learn that people's body weights pull against and push off from each other in order to get the strongest effect. Your ability to help the girl you're partnering depends a great deal upon your understanding of weight distribution.

In partnering in ballet, I find that more often than not,

rather than the man manipulating the woman, the man takes his lead from the woman. In classical ballet, the woman is the central focus; the man's concern is to show her off. Yet together they must create an aura of romance. In contemporary ballet and modern dance, it's nearly completely equal. I think that's evident in Jerry Robbins' ballets, for example. There's a great deal of counterbalancing off the standing leg. Usually things are pulled out, or leaning over. They're not straight up and down. In his ballets the partnering is trickier than most and it's helpful to have more than the average partnering ability. Classical ballet is more vertical-horizontal in feeling.

When I joined ABT, I was very thin and weak, like a little pony. I had to do Glen Tetley's *Voluntaries* with Elaine Kudo. The ballet had very difficult lifts: for example, one where the man supports the woman by the waist with one hand and under the leg with the other, and lifts her in an open scissor position over his head.

Another particularly hard step comes at the end of a long section where, as the couple run, the man lifts the woman by bracing both his hands at the back of her waist as she splits her legs in a grand jeté, and he presses her up over his head as they exit off stage. I would invariably get Elaine up, but not *all* the way up, and she would slowly sink down on top of my head and as I carried her off! My "head lifts" became a running joke in that ballet. I never thought I would become a good partner because, in the beginning, I couldn't lift very well.

Voluntaries was the hardest partnering ballet for the corps de ballet, otherwise there wasn't too much challenging partnering for the corps. When I started getting thrown into more and more ballets and having to work really hard, I never made a conscious effort to study partnering. It was something that became necessary in order to perform those ballets.

Partnering is something that can make you feel very competent or incompetent. If you have trouble in a partnering relationship with a woman, it becomes a struggle, a fight between partners. You become insecure and your responsiveness becomes strained. It's timing. It's all in the timing. If you work at it, you can learn to adjust your timing. As I began to perform more ballets, I began to develop my sense of timing and to realize that I had a certain ability to feel where my partner should be, how much I should touch her.

In a pirouette, for example, some girls like to be pushed around as they turn, others don't like any force at all. You're only there to stop them at the end. That's something you must sense. Some girls can do multiple pirouettes and stay on pointe all by themselves. Others have a hard time turning, so you have to help them. It was fascinating for me to discover how each girl was so completely different that I had to *feel* exactly when she was going to take off or go up on her pointes, or sense when and how much she wanted to be turned. Holding is equally variable. Some girls take hold of you strongly, as if they're shaking your hand. The touch of others is very light and soft.

For example when a girl does a piqué arabesque and takes your hand for a promenade, you either feel a driving connection with that person, or you feel only the slightest touch. Personally, I like to feel a tension with my partners because I can feel what's happening between us. A light touch can be very misleading. However, there should never look like there is tension. It should look as soft and effortless as possible.

Cynthia Gregory is very strong and things come very naturally to her. She's the kind of ballerina who doesn't really need much help. You just have to be there to sustain the flow of the choreography. The challenge of dancing with Cynthia is not to get in her way. I did *Coppélia* with her and there were several big lifts in our pas de deux. When we started rehearsals, she offered to change things such as the overhead press lift. But I didn't want to change anything. I wanted to do the choreography as it was supposed to be done.

I knew she was conscious of being a big partner for me and was trying to be thoughtful. But I was persistent. I saw it as a challenge to be able to lift Cynthia Gregory over my head. I didn't want her performance to be faulted because of my inability. Interestingly, when she prepares to be lifted, her timing is so deliberate, you know exactly when to lift. When that preparation is there, it makes all the difference and it becomes much easier to lift her. She also *really* jumps on every lift. I suppose she has acquired these helpful traits from having more than her fair share of trouble throughout her career in finding the right partner.

I learned through experience that partnering is very similar to weight lifting. A weight lifter takes a very deep plié, or knee-bend, lifts the weight to chest level, then straightens his legs as he presses the weight up over his head with his arms. Partnering in ballet is very similar. The secret of a successful lift is that much of it is done with the legs. If the timing is right as you lift, and the legs are straightened simultaneously with the arms, the legs give the arms an extra boost of thrusting power. In partnering Cynthia, I also found that since she is tall, her waist was already so high, so close to my navel, that I only had to take a short plié and lift her to eye level.

Oddly enough, it's often more difficult to partner shorter girls, because you have to lift them a further distance to get the same effect. For example, Gelsey Kirkland is very hard to lift. At top weight, she might be 95 pounds to Cynthia's 125. But when Gelsey prepared for a lift, she never jumped for you. Her weight went *down,* as if pulled by gravity. She pushed down, and instead of breathing in, she exhaled. So, when her partner lifts, it creates the illusion of her body being lifted in slow motion by an external force. It is actually very beautiful to watch, but very difficult on her partner. She would just point her feet, not helping her partner by pushing up into a lift, which made it all the more difficult.

In September, 1982, I did Act II *Giselle* with Gelsey for Edward Villella and the Eglevsky Ballet at Hofstra University in Hempstead, Long Island. Gelsey was scheduled to dance three *Giselles* there with Patrick Bissell, the third of which was to be performed the weekend after the first two, but he had injured his back during the week. This was during what was probably Gelsey's worse period of cocaine abuse. She had had one of her seizures shortly before. She saw me in class and asked me if I would replace Patrick. I was flattered and without giving it much thought said I would.

We had two rehearsals for that performance. She showed up about an hour late for the first one, and we barely got through half of the act before she had to go. The second rehearsal, we did perhaps three-quarters of the Act. The day of the performance, we rehearsed as well. She was wearing pointe shoes that were as thin as tissue paper, they had no support left in them. She was very patient, but she was also, I believe, very high and distracted. She constantly ran to the phone, "checking on things." But she was patient with me because she knew at this point that this was her only chance at fulfilling the engagement.

Eddie Villella picked me up on the day of the performance to drive us to Hempstead. When we picked Gelsey up, her hair was still the same way it had been during the two rehearsals we had. She looked like she hadn't slept for about five days—her skin was white and grainy and at this point she was very, very thin, probably weighing no more than eighty-five pounds. We didn't get very far before she had to stop at a drugstore on Seventy-second Street because, she mumbled, she had to pick up makeup, which I seriously wondered about. We resumed heading out of the city and, chain-smoking all the way, Gelsey went off on a tangent about her childhood and her father.

Gelsey would often go off on tangents. I remember one rehearsal for *Gottschalk* that turned into a therapy session with me. She wanted someone to talk to. She told me how cruel her father had been, wanting her and her sister Johnna to be models. As children, they were photographed and their father forced them to smile. She said she obeyed, but it was a cruel smile. From that time, she hated to be told to smile. She hated the very word. During that rehearsal she opened herself up to me. She told me about her analyst, about a beautiful girl she had met at a hospital drug rehabilitation program who reminded her of Sophia Loren, how they became good friends. She told me how this girl had been treated cruelly and had learned to trick the doctors and frequently escaped. I stood listening, not knowing why Gelsey, who I hardly knew, would be telling me all this, but that was the way she was. As we drove, I kept thinking, I'm going to do a performance with someone in this condition; this far gone?

We got to Hofstra, and Gelsey retreated to her dressing room almost immediately after our arrival. We were trying to find her to rehearse and discovered she had decided to take a nap. I did a barre by myself. About thirty minutes before curtain time, I went to Gelsey's dressing room, knocked on the door and said, "Gelsey, I think we should figure out what we're going to do for the end of the second act." Luckily, I had performed *Giselle* with Cynthia Harvey, and it was basically the same version that Gelsey had done with Patrick, which she had originally done with Misha. But the ending was always different, usually depending on the ballerina's choice, and I hated the thought of going on cold, without having the ending worked out.

Ten minutes before curtain time, there we were on stage rehearsing what we were going to perform within an hour's time. She couldn't make up her mind which lift she wanted to do. Then, without coming to any definite conclusion, she disappeared to get dressed for the performance. I stood there thinking, Well, I guess we'll just have to make it up when we get there. I finally laughed nervously to myself, This is certainly going to be the most interesting performance I've ever been a part of! As I walked slowly back to my dressing room, the seriousness of the situation began to hit me with full force. What had I gotten myself into? Was this for real? I knew one thing. This would be the first and last performance I would decide to go through with solely for the money. Getting to my dressing room, I closed the door behind me, leaned back against it, rolled my eyes heavenward, sighed deeply and thought, Marsha Woody *never* said there'd be days like *this*!

The curtain went up and we made our entrances. When we came together and I took her hand, she was shaking from head to toe. She was having great difficulty staying on pointe and gripped my hand so tightly I thought she might draw blood. And this was only the opening of the pas de deux. In her développées, she would lean back to the point where I thought she'd fall over. I held onto her as tightly as I could, to let her know she wouldn't have to do it on her own. The whole thing was wild and wonky, very unpredictable, totally unlike the calculated performances I had come to expect from her, and bore no resemblance to our rehearsals.

The performance seemed to deteriorate as Gelsey got weaker and weaker. I was so tired from trying to keep her from falling that I felt too exhausted for my variation. As it was, I was out of shape since this performance took place during a layoff, and I had been off for two weeks. It was probably the worst variation I have ever done. But I didn't care. I was more concerned about trying to prevent Gelsey from falling down or flipping out.

At the end of the Act, there's an option of doing what is called a "cradle lift" or another overhead press, which is what she wanted. We made it through to the end and did the overhead lift. She felt like she weighed 150 pounds. It was the most difficult lift of my career. When I put her down, she headed in a different direction than what we rehearsed. At this point, Giselle is supposed to be disappearing into the grave as Albrecht, reaching for her, can no longer see her. Suddenly, the moment became real. I was so desperate to finish, I almost panicked. I was scared and wanted the curtain to come down. Finally, she disappeared and, relieved, I wondered if this *Giselle* had made any sense at all to the audience.

The curtain came down, and I thought of calling a hospital to come and take her away. Gelsey had exhausted herself. Instead of saving her strength, she did the performance as full out as if she were doing it with Misha at the Met. I think one of the reasons she gave so much was for Eddie. During that ride in the car, she spoke about him with absolute admiration, remembering how wonderful he was in *Prodigal Son,* how when she saw him do it she cried. Backstage, Gelsey thanked me for the performance, almost as if it were a business deal. She must have been happy just to have gotten through it. So was I.

Cynthia Harvey was the easiest ballerina to partner of any I ever danced with. Our ways of moving, our timing and coordination were very similar. I knew this from the very first time I worked with her, and it could be dangerous. When you work with someone who is so like yourself, your dancing together can look too natural, too coordinated. There's no friction or edge. So, with Cynthia, I always tried to take our dancing to the limit. Instead of making it feel right, I tried making it a little harder for her by not partnering her as much. Since she was very strong, she would always compensate, with exciting results.

One of the few ballerinas, along with Cynthia Gregory, to rise through the ranks of ABT from corps to principal under Lucia, Marianna Tcherkassky was another delight to work with. Marianna was primarily partnered by Misha, Danilo Radojevic and Johan Renvall, so we were rarely cast together.

But as it turned out, I danced with her often by replacing her scheduled partners in ballets such as *La Sylphide, Cinderella, Giselle* and *Romeo and Juliet.* A warm, raven-haired, dark-eyed beauty, Marianna is very easy to work with because she's so good-natured. She's ethereally light and her lovely, curved hips accent her waist, which is tiny enough for your hands to fit around perfectly. Partnering her is a dream.

If Cynthia and Marianna were two of the easiest ballerinas to partner, Susan Jaffe was the most difficult. She has amazing extension and an extraordinary back that curves into her rear like an "S." It's beautiful to look at, but it's difficult to feel where her weight is over her leg, or where she wants to be. I always had trouble responding to her physically. On the other hand, she knew exactly how to explain what she wanted. She could feel it; she could tell you. She could even explain what she needed in terms of timing. In a way, it was intimidating. Being given instructions on what is needed gives a male partner the feeling he's not really in control of the situation.

Great Galloping Gottschalk was made for me and Susan Jaffe, but Lynne Taylor-Corbett actually created most of it for herself and a dancer friend. For the most part, it was already done by the time she taught it to us. Susan and I did that ballet so many times it was like brushing teeth. Despite the fact that other than *Other Dances* we didn't dance much together, among fans we became something of a "partnership." I suppose it was because our careers in ABT started to emerge at the same time and we received a lot of press together.

When I think about Susan, I can't help but think about pulling a "Susan Jaffe" or, I would hope, *not* pulling one. Susan has a wonderfully endearing, if embarrassing knack for saying the wrong thing at the wrong time. We'd go to a fancy party at a wealthy patron's house, and she'd say something like, "The apartment is beautiful but the food is *awful!*" Inevitably, the hostess would be standing directly behind her. That's a

"Susan Jaffe." Thankfully, we've developed ways to steer her away from a lot of situations before she can pull one, although as Susan knows, I've had my share of "Susan Jaffes."

I did *Prodigal* and *Jardin aux Lilas* with Martine van Hamel. I never understood why dancing with Martine never felt any different on stage than it did in rehearsal. She was one of the few partners I never felt that change in. You didn't have to react or respond to the unexpected—she's so placed and under control that a partner knows exactly what he's getting on stage. But there's a flip side to this: I never felt Martine took chances with a partner or trusted me enough to put herself in my hands. Perhaps it was our chemistry or the fact that she was much taller than me. She's a big woman, big-boned, with beautiful musculature, feet and legs, torso; everything very well proportioned.

Leslie Browne, on the other hand, is like a roller-coaster ride at an amusement park. "Fun" is the word for Leslie. You have to be constantly alert with her. She can take a pique arabesque as if she could explode at any second. I used to call her "kamikaze on pointe." I was very fortunate to have her as my Juliet, because she gave it a different dimension. She was a young woman trying to break out of her shell. She was anything but the clichéd, romantic, fawning puppy-love young thing. She gave the role a great deal of force and sexual urgency. But she would take risks that were actually scary. There's a lift in *Romeo and Juliet* where she comes running, then turns her back to me and jumps in the air as I catch and lift her. Kenneth wanted her to jump from very far away. Well, the very first time we did it, I was at quarter mark and she turned and jumped from center stage! But if she did it from a point any closer, I found it was much harder for me to lift her. Leslie has an amazing jump. I think she can jump higher than any male dancer—except perhaps Misha. She's as buoyant as a pogo stick and you never know what she might do.

Amanda McKerrow dances the way she looks. She's well-mannered, pretty and neat. She's a very kind person with a lovely, tender quality. She has one of those techniques that allows her to do anything, almost as though she didn't need a partner. She's an independent kind of person and an independent kind of dancer. She can take care of herself. As Juliet, she was more innocent than Leslie. Her Juliet was a young girl discovering things for the first time about her womanliness. She's a very well trained dancer. She made everything she had to do look very easy. In fact, everything was easy to do with her. I never felt anything could go wrong. Except once. One of my funniest performance experiences happened with Amanda. I was dancing *Romeo and Juliet* with her in Miami. We came to kiss at the end of the pas de deux, and I didn't realize that because she was breathing so heavily, she had her mouth wide-open. I went to kiss her with my lips and stuck my face in her mouth!

Chapter 14

DURING ABT's 1985 Spring tour, I had begun to take assessment of my life. I thought a lot about how much I wished I could spend more time in New York with my friends. I was sick of the pattern of just getting used to being around a group of people and then leaving them to spend four or more months on the road. Of course, I had friends in the company, but I immediately spent less time with them whenever I returned to New York.

More importantly, the long and frequent touring had begun to take its toll on my relationship with Steven. Distance made it difficult for us to share friends, social events and to have the necessary time alone together. This is a frequent problem and recurrent theme in many dancers' lives. It's one of the reasons dancers often develop personal relationships within the company.

Steven was still deeply involved in his computerized nutritional analyzing program with his friend and partner, Dr. Barry Gingell, and would spend hours at the library doing research. The ultimate goal was to establish their own company, O.N.E.—Optimal Nutrition Engineering. Steven and Barry eventually found an office and opened for business, which was slow at first.

After a while, Barry developed sores in his mouth known as

Thrush. Being a doctor, Barry knew they were a symptom of AIDS. He became sicker and sicker, eventually developed pneumonia and had to be taken to the hospital. At the time little was known about AIDS.

Fear ran rampant. It was reported that the virus was found even in saliva. But Barry assured us it was transmitted by blood and semen and, as far as we were concerned, only through sexual contact. I remember going to visit him in the hospital for the first time. I was nervous, terrified really, of being in the same room, let alone touching him. Oddly enough, he didn't look sick at all. In fact, he was in a rather chipper mood, laughing as we played *Trivial Pursuit,* and waiting to get out of the hospital. About a week later, Barry was out of the hospital and continued to see patients. He diagnosed several cases of AIDS.

I became increasingly worried. I thought every little spot on my body was Kaposi's Sarcoma. Paranoia set in. And with good reason. AIDS was being reported as the exclusive disease of gays and drug users. Conversations among many of our friends always led to the same subject, frustration with the ignorant and arrogant attitudes of government and society. We heard of men dying and morgues refusing to embalm them. Human beings were being thrown into the trash.

The business wasn't going well and anticipating Barry's unavoidable medical bills and the care he would need, Steven asked him to move in with us in order to save the expense of rent on an apartment. He slept in the living room. Steven started to devote a great deal of time to Barry, which was understandable considering the state of his health. But Steven's and my limited time together now revolved around Barry.

Steven and Barry began to make plans. Barry knew of two drugs, Ribovirin and Isoprinisin, that were said to be effective in boosting the immune system. They were easily obtainable as over-the-counter drugs in Mexico but hadn't yet been approved by the Food and Drug Administration in the United States. These drugs hadn't been tested for their effectiveness in fighting the AIDS virus, but Barry decided to use himself as a guinea pig. They flew to California, rented a car and drove across the border to "buy out" the drug stores in Tijuana. Writers from *People* magazine got wind of it, followed Steven and Barry on their mission and a story appeared in *People* the following week.

Soon after Steven returned from Mexico, he had trouble sleeping. I could tell by the way he was relating to me that it wasn't Barry's illness alone that was bothering him. He didn't talk as much as he had in the past. Was it something I had done? Was he bored with me? Was there someone else? Was I losing him? I couldn't separate one thought from another, let alone think straight. Steven was definitely trying to tell me something, but I simply wasn't getting the message. Sometimes I wished he'd just come out and say, "It's over. I don't love you anymore." I told myself I could handle it and move on.

One night after dinner, Steven and I were lying in bed watching T.V. I noticed he seemed to be staring right through the television and was obviously deep in thought. I pretended to fall asleep. A while later, he turned off the T.V. The bedroom windows were open and moonlight filtered in through the wooden shutters. A cool breeze swept over my face. I felt I could almost "hear" Steven's thoughts. I knew he was about to speak.

"Robby, are you asleep?" he whispered.

"No. What is it? What's wrong?"

"It's so hard to explain. I'm not sure you'll understand."

I couldn't say a thing, fearing I knew what he was about to say. The rest of the conversation was filled with long silences. They were as meaningful as the words.

"Robby, I didn't want this to happen. It's not you. I just feel

181

like we've become a habit with each other. I don't have the freedom I thought I'd have with you."

I understood what he was saying. I could relate to what he was feeling because I was beginning to feel it, too. After a year or so of living in such an intimate relationship with Steven, I had begun to think of everything in my life in terms of how it affected *two* people, not one. I felt the need for an independence I had never had. Nevertheless, I had become *dependent* on Steven and didn't want him to slip through my fingers.

"I suppose it would be best for me to move out, then," I said, finally. After another of those long pauses he said, "Well, yes. But it will probably be better, Robby. We can see each other whenever we really want to, not just because we live together." He wanted to have the choice. I understood and told myself it didn't matter whether I lived with him or not. I loved him and didn't want to lose the relationship. If he had asked me at the time to move to Timbuktu, I would have said yes.

A week later I moved out. My apartment on 71st Street was sublet, so I couldn't return there.

Peter Fonseca owned a huge loft on 38th Street that had an extra bedroom, and he said I could move in with him. I wanted everyone to think I was handling the crisis rather maturely. On the surface, everything seemed like normal. But inside I was crumbling. I felt like a vagabond. For the fifth time in seven years—five years if you subtract all the time I spent on tour—I had everything I owned in a van needing a place to live. On top of that, I couldn't bear the feeling of being rejected. Who can?

Days began to feel like weeks, months like years. I didn't understand what was happening to me or exactly what it was that I was feeling. It wasn't just Steven. Depression? I asked myself. No, not me! I had everything I had always wanted, a successful career in one of the world's great dance companies, a certain amount of celebrity, and the beginning of a new

aspect of my artistic self through choreography. But everywhere I looked, I saw only the negative in my life.

I hated *Requiem*, the new ballet Kenneth MacMillan was
choreographing, and thought the Andrew Lloyd Webber
music was terrible and cheap. The choreography uninspired. I
knew it would be a failure. Besides, I wasn't Misha's understudy this time around. I was a secondary lead. The one
bright spot was being cast with Leslie Browne as my partner.
Another choreographer, Karole Armitage, this sort of
"punked-out" ballet dancer with an incredible understanding
of ballet, was creating a new ballet for Misha, Leslie and me. I
was enjoying the experience as much as I could, considering I
wasn't doing the part I wanted—Misha's. Karole told me I
could learn his part if I wanted, but I still had trouble concentrating and giving 100 percent.

Something was definitely wrong. I couldn't believe what
my brain seemed to be telling me. Was I suddenly too grand
to dance behind Mikhail Baryshnikov?! After all, he was my
idol, my hero, my mentor. The greatest male dancer in the
world. I knew I should feel privileged to be even in the same
rehearsal room, let alone to share the stage with him. But I
was so *unhappy*, so frustrated and confused.

I finally had to let Charles know how dissatisfied I was with
Requiem and that my life in general seemed so miserable. But
even with Charles, my artistic confidant, I couldn't tell the
whole truth. Something was preventing me from letting him
in on what was really on my mind. This time around, I was
thinking, I *really* wanted to call it quits.

I had spent months of sleepless nights trying to figure out
how I would survive without a weekly paycheck. I would go
back to commercials, or I might try to get back in a show
(*Song and Dance* had just opened on Broadway), or I'd wait on
tables if I had to. What else was I prepared to do? What did I
really want to do? I had no idea. I didn't know where to turn.
Lola Herman, my astrologer friend, saw my future in chore-

ography. "Fine," I thought, "that's it. I'll just choreograph, anything, for any civic company that will have me." In my own way, I prayed. But it was obvious God wasn't going to send a telegram with the answer.

And then again, I thought, what about my dancing? Could I actually leave behind the last ten years of my life? Was I ready, willing, or able to stop dancing altogether? Part of me said I couldn't, but I couldn't rid myself of this debilitating confusion. The most I could say to myself was that I didn't want to break down, "cop out" or give in. I was struggling to "hang in there" and at least see the next year through.

I needed answers that I felt neither I nor my friends could provide. Could I stand another four month tour? I doubted it. I foresaw the strong possibility of turning to drugs in order to survive. Maybe cocaine was the answer. That's when I knew I needed professional help.

Through friends, I found out about Laurel Morris, an analyst. I called and made an appointment. I didn't have a problem with the idea of seeing an analyst—I was actually intrigued by the idea that there were people who professionally deal with the problems of other people. But I was nervous about what exactly was expected of me. I walked into her apartment, which was tastefully decorated, and was greeted by a slender, attractive lady in a Laura Ashley print dress. So this was the analyst.

I sat down in a big rocking chair and waited for her to start. I stared at her. A minute went by. I kept staring. Two minutes went by. Still staring. I looked out the window for a moment, then turned and stared for another three minutes. I finally sat back and relaxed, wondering what sort of game this was. Was she waiting for me to get unnerved? Suddenly, I felt I could see myself in her eyes, as if I were staring into a mirror. I realized this session was about *me* and if I didn't say something soon, nothing would be said.

I thought I'd test her to see if she'd break before I would, but realized the futility of that idea.

Finally, I laughed. "What's all this about?" I asked.

She said, "Do you have anything to say?"

"Of course, I do," I answered, "but I don't know how to start."

"You can start by telling me about yourself. What's going on?"

I told her about myself, my dancing, who I was associated with, my relationships and what I was going through. An hour passed and I realized that she hadn't said a word. I had done all the talking and at the same time, I was listening to what I was saying. I heard my own words as another person might hear them and realized she was letting me hear myself objectively.

She closed the session by telling me to write down any dreams I might have and tell her about them in the next session. Through the next several weeks, we didn't talk about my life in chronological order, although Laurel occasionally asked me something about my childhood.

"As a child, I was always afraid to go to bed. I was afraid of the dark. I used to try to sleep by myself until I just couldn't take it. I was always afraid my father would think I was a weakling, but I couldn't help it. I would go to my parents' bedroom and timidly ask, 'Mom, would you come stay with me until I fall asleep?' She'd get up, go back to my room and sit with me until I drifted off. I did this until I was twelve or thirteen. I was definitely afraid of something. I didn't want to be alone.

"My fear was about being alone in a room; alone in a room in the dark with a window and a closet with closed doors. It had something to do with intruders coming in through the windows, or breaking down the doors. I was afraid that someone was going to get me. All the boys had a room

185

together with bunkbeds, and as long as Harold and Edmund were there it was all right. But when Harold, and then Edmund, left, that's when it started to happen. I was afraid to be alone. When I first moved to New York, I lived with Edmund, then Kenneth roomed with me. On tour I always had a roommate. Then I lived with Steven. When we broke up, I moved into Peter Fonseca's loft. I made sure I was never alone."

In a later session, I told Laurel about one of my dreams.

"It was night. A man came into the loft. He had a knife. At first I was frightened, but I jumped up, overpowered him, took the knife and beat him up."

In describing the dream, I realized that I could overcome my fear by attacking the source of it. I recognized my long-standing need to learn how to live on my own. After that, it gradually got better. I live alone now. I don't think anymore about the front door and somebody breaking in.

In other sessions, I found I just had to discuss my feelings about my brother Edmund.

"When I first came to New York, Edmund and I shared an apartment for three or four months until I went on tour with ABT. He was dancing with Eliot Feld. In fact he was the star of the company. Eliot was creating most of his new works on Edmund.

"Edmund was into Nichiren Shoshu Buddhism and chanted every morning and night. I was quite intrigued by it. I went to meetings with him and listened to what they had to say. They believed you could chant for things that you want. I tried it, but I got really tired. I got winded and out of breath. It felt so ancient and ritualistic to me that I couldn't relate to it. It was something I had no connection with. I found no meditative benefits in chanting. It didn't work for me, but it was something Edmund believed in and I respected that. It was wonderful to see that Edmund had something to focus on. At the time, I was focusing on my social life.

"Then Edmund started to have problems with Eliot. He was getting tired of Eliot and they would have fights. He would complain about how hard he was to work with. So he started going out to Studio 54 with us and he stopped chanting. I really saw a change in Edmund. He replaced one force in his life with another, and it was bad for him.

"He became obsessed with going out. It started detracting from his job. He'd miss rehearsals or be late. I can't say he stopped going to class, because he always did his own barre. He rarely took a ballet class from another teacher. I never could do my own class. It was always too hard to motivate myself. I need someone in front of me telling me what to do. That's the only way it works for me, so I have a hard time understanding how Edmund could go in every day and do his own class. But he could. He worked harder that way.

"Anyway, when Misha took over ABT and I started to be used in ballets and have success, Edmund's career started taking a slide. It was very hard for me to see my older brother, the hero of my youth, struggling. There were times when I somehow felt responsible, that there was something that I could do. But I don't think there was anything anyone could do.

"Edmund tried many times to get over his problems, but I think his real problem was New York. He couldn't deal with it. As long as Edmund was working with Eliot Feld or in *Dancin'*, which he did, like me, he was fine. He got into trouble when he wasn't working. Being in New York and having nothing to do, not having somewhere to focus all your attention, can get you into a lot of trouble. You can also get very bored. It's hard when you have nothing to do, and also when you're not making any money. Fortunately, I guess, I was never in that situation.

"Edmund's problem certainly wasn't a carryover from his childhood in Beaumont. It was basically that he had nothing to focus his attention on. He wanted to dance very much.

Twyla Tharp was interested in considering him for her company. He was supposed to talk to Twyla, but he got nervous and never showed up for the talk.

"Then he joined Les Grands Ballets Canadiens. That lasted about six months before he sustained an injury. He didn't like it there anyway. I think he liked the company and the dancers, but he didn't like the climate. He said it was too cold in Montreal. So he came back to New York with nothing to do and lived with me for a month.

"I didn't think it was healthy for him to hang out for a month, so I asked him what he was going to do next. He was recovering from an injury, but he was spending all his money staying in New York when he could have gone home to Beaumont. He just didn't want to go home, and stayed with me at Peter Fonseca's loft. He had nothing to do, so he wanted to go out and party every night. One night he came home late drunk, and knocked over one of Peter's beautiful glass pieces. I never had the heart to tell Peter. Another time he knocked over a bottle of cologne, and the bathroom stunk for days.

"He finally did go home. At first, he had trouble adjusting. But then he started working out, taking class with Marsha Woody in Beaumont and getting his act together. Marsha contacted Robert Barnett in Atlanta Ballet, and they offered him a job. Edmund took it and with good results.

"He's been with Atlanta Ballet the longest of all his jobs since Eliot. He has an apartment. He's done all of his performances. He's become almost suburban. He seems to have accepted the fact that he doesn't have to go racing around the world, that Atlanta will be just fine. I love my brother, and I'm happy for him. It's nice for him to have gotten to that point."

Discussions with Laurel came around to Steven and our break-up. I talked about the situation with Barry, AIDS, and Steven's need to be independent. I told her that I was beginning to realize that his suggestion that it would be "better" was not what I originally took it to mean; that as weeks passed, we had been seeing less and less of each other. I felt hurt, rejected, deceived. "I've tried to understand," I said, "to see it from his point of view, but I still feel so dependent on him, and he seems to be so independent of me, that I can't help feeling that I've been rejected. I guess I have to face the inevitable. It's over. It's too bad, because God knows I still care."

The sessions continued—even though I couldn't believe the amount of money I was spending to listen to myself talk—and I also wrote down all of my dreams, one of which Laurel helped me discover was showing me feelings I had about ABT that I hadn't been able to address consciously.

"Charles, Susan Jones and Elaine Kudo, my friends in ABT, and I were leaving for a party. Misha drove up in a beautiful, gleaming white Rolls-Royce. He asked us to join him, and I was the last to get in the car. Just as I was about to hop in, the door slammed and Misha drove off, but not before I managed to climb onto the back of the car. The car raced along at a hundred miles an hour, with me clinging onto the fender for dear life. They were all laughing, especially Misha. Finally, I became so frightened, I simply let go and flew off. I found myself floating gently, effortlessly, and softly bounced into a two-foot-deep carpet of rich green grass. Lying there, I looked into the night and saw the taillights of the car disappear into the darkness. I turned and saw a policeman with a flashlight walking in my direction. I hid in the tall grass and he walked on by without seeing me."

Although Laurel analyzed the dream for me, I basically figured it out for myself. I was feeling shut out from the ABT fold and was desperately clinging on. But when I let go, I would feel free. I had escaped from what was supposed to be "right" according to "the law" (the policeman). More than anything

189

else, I was afraid of approaching Misha. I was terrified of hearing his "yes" *or* his "no." I was afraid of doing what I had to do. It wasn't a question of being right or wrong. I was intimidated by the authority figures, people in power. I had already figured out the answer to what I wanted to do with my life, but I was having trouble dealing with it.

Laurel wasn't the only person I spoke to about the crisis in my life. Gary Lisz was my best friend and provided more than just a sympathetic ear.

A graduate of Parsons School of Design in New York, Gary immediately made it big on Seventh Avenue and at one point had two lines of his designs at the best stores in New York, as well as his own boutique at Bloomingdale's. But it wasn't enough. He wasn't in control of his own life. He had a hard time dealing with the problem and finally made the decision to give it all up and chop vegetables if he had to—and for a while, he did. He knew that what he really wanted was to study fine art, and eventually he attended the Corcoran Institute in Washington, D.C., for two and a half years, and was happy.

It was October 1985. Gary and I were with friends at a Halloween party for ABT at Visage, a West Side nightclub. I was having a very hard time coping with the setting and the crowd that night. "You know, Gary, something's seriously wrong," I said as we left. "I hate the feeling of going all the way down to Nineteenth Street every day, the feeling of being at home in New York for only eight weeks and on the road for months at a time, the feeling of not really knowing where I am, the feeling of not having a home base. I'm not grounded. I'm a gypsy. I can't deal with being a gypsy. It's a scary feeling but I would *love* to quit ABT.

"I'm not mad at anyone. I don't even blame anyone. I know I have everything I ever wanted in my life, but it's not enough. I just don't want my life to be a dead end. I don't want to be at ABT at thirty-five, contemplating my retirement and not knowing what to do with my life. I want to be in control. I want to be with my friends, work on our projects, choreograph. I don't know, Gary, but for the first time in my life, I think I know what I *really* want."

For most of my life, I wanted to do what I thought would please others—my parents, Marsha Woody, my teachers, my artistic directors. Now, I wanted to grow up, even if I made a mistake. The point was taking a chance. I didn't want to do the "safe" thing anymore.

"I'll work at the A&P if I have to," I continued. "I'll do anything as long as it's a change."

"Boy, you *are* serious!" Gary said to me. "But I know *exactly* what you're talking about. You already know what you have to do."

"What's that?"

"Leave already. Take a vacation from success!"

Admittedly, if it hadn't been for Misha, I wouldn't have had a career. But it was past history, one had to grow, move on . . . I told Charles that I was having trouble dealing with everything in my life, including my work and that I felt I wanted to leave, had to leave. He clearly didn't want to accept it. I went to Florence Pettan and told her I had to talk to Misha privately and that it would take more than sitting down for five minutes. She made the appointment, and Misha and I went to lunch around the corner from the ABT studios.

"Okay, what's going on?" he asked as we sat down. "I can tell there's something really bothering you. You've been acting very strange."

He was referring to an incident that had happened during a *Requiem* rehearsal. Kenneth MacMillan was going very slowly and making frequent changes. There were three sets of principals in the room all doing the same steps. Finding it hard to focus, Leslie and I started talking to each other. I had gotten to a point where I was laughing at everything. I had just choreographed *Rappaccini's Daughter* for Leslie, and we were having too good of a time in rehearsal. Catching us off guard, Kenneth asked us to demonstrate the next step, and we didn't know it. He understandably got very upset and lit into me.

"What is your *problem*?" he demanded.

"*Nothing* is my problem," I snapped. "I don't *have* a problem."

"Then why are you acting up?"

"You keep changing the step. I don't know *what* it is!" Not wanting to make any more of a scene, I said, "I'm sorry." Kenneth *knew* then that something was wrong.

I told Misha during lunch that I was having a serious problem focusing, that I was having trouble going on tour, that I was having doubts about myself in classical ballets. I didn't know why. I did know that I couldn't continue being in the company at that time.

"What is it, Robby? What do you want?" Misha asked with genuine concern. "Can I take you out of some ballets?"

"It has nothing to do with what I'm dancing, Misha. You've given me everything I could ever want to dance. It's my own self-doubts. I can't even really explain to you why. Along with everything else," I told him, "Steven has left me."

"Don't worry," he assured me, "it will pass. You'll get over that." Perhaps that was true, but at that point I couldn't deal with it along with everything else and remain with the company.

Though caught completely offguard and upset by the news, Misha recovered quickly and told me he understood that I had to do what I felt and that as a friend he had to respect that. He said he'd have to talk to John Taras and Kenneth MacMillan, his artistic associates, and see what needed to be done to replace me on tour. He asked me when I planned to leave. I had already rehearsed for my debut as the Prince in *The Nutcracker*, so I said I would stay until the end of the Christmas-week performances in L.A. He said "Fine," which was all he really could say.

A week went by and it became common knowledge that I was leaving the company, but many dancers thought it was merely rumor. In fact, when I confirmed the rumor, they still didn't believe me. They thought I was joking.

Another week went by and Misha had to talk to me. He told me that an all-Tudor evening was planned for the up-coming season and that Tudor had no one else to dance *Jardin aux Lilas,* since Kevin McKenzie was already cast in *The Leaves are Fading* and *Dim Lustre.* He asked me to reconsider.

"I've already made so many plans, Misha," I told him. "I've gone this far and I just can't turn back." I begged him to try to work it out some other way. He said he would tell Mr. Tudor.

By this time, Charles was in shock. He couldn't accept that I was really going to leave. He told me the company would have a terribly hard time on tour without me. I understood their need for leading male dancers, since Fernando had left the company several months earlier. On the other hand, I reasoned that if I were injured, they would have to find someone to replace me. Dancers get injured all the time, and the company has to be prepared to deal with it.

Kenneth asked me to keep coming to rehearsals for *Requiem.* He wanted to continue working on a pas de deux he was creating for Leslie and me that he considered "very Balanchine." I didn't find it terribly "Balanchine." I had liked the first version best, which was the most interesting. I continued to go to those rehearsals, and I taught John Gardner my part in David Gordon's ballet *Murder.*

Meanwhile, choreographer Karole Armitage was trying her hardest to get me to meet the company on tour just to do a secondary lead in her ballet *The Mollino Room.* She had really taken a liking to me and we had great rapport. It seemed she just didn't want anyone else in the part: I thanked her for wanting me in her ballet so much, but doubted that the company would approve the arrangement, even if I had wanted to do it. I started teaching *Mollino Room* to Ricardo Bustamante and could see what Karole meant. When a choreographer makes a ballet on a specific dancer, there are things that dancer does that are uniquely his or her own. When a choreographer becomes accustomed to seeing those characteristics in the movement, it's difficult to adapt to a new person. Later, within the context of the whole piece and when the ballet takes on a life of its own through performance, it's different.

Back in *Requiem* rehearsals another principal dancer, Clark Tippet, was learning my part, and Gil Boggs, a soloist, was replacing Misha, who was injured. Essentially, much of Misha's part was worked out on Gil with Alessandra Ferri, and Gil eventually premiered the ballet. Had I stayed, I would have been one of six principals, dancing behind a soloist. I had gotten to the point where something like that bothered me. I found it hard to take. Anything I could find to pick on, I did, to boost my faltering ego.

Peter Fonseca supported my decision to leave. He had known for some time that there was something wrong, that I was unhappy. Anyone who knew me knew I had an interest in Broadway, commercials, acting and choreography. They knew I wasn't a complete "bunhead." Peter was excited for me. No one, in fact, except for Charles, had any opposing opinion, simply because I was so strong willed about my decision. Nothing that anyone said could sway me. When someone makes a decision like that, whatever the consequences, there's nothing *anyone* can say.

"Yearning to be free . . ." as the "Prodigal Son" with (l to r) Antonia Franceschi, Adam Lüders, Deborah Wingert, (NYCB, 1986). (Photo by Paul Kolnik)

My debut in *Prodigal Son* with Cynthia Gregory as "the Siren." (ABT, 1980). (Photo by Martha Swope)

With Martine van Hamel as the "Siren." (ABT). (Photo by Mira)

Seduced by Darci Kistler as the "Siren." (NYCB, 1986). (Photo by Paul Kolnik)

With Merrill Ashley as the "Siren." (NYCB, 1986). (Photo by Paul Kolnik)

"At their mercy . . ." (NYCB, 1986). (Photo by Paul Kolnik)

Darci Kistler, "The Siren Triumphant," (NYCB, 1986). (Photo by Paul Kolnik)

"Robbed, stripped naked, and abandoned . . ." (NYCB). (Photo by Paul Kolnik)

". . . pleading for help . . ." (ABT). (Photo by Monroe Warshaw)

". . . the kindness of my sisters . . ." with Antonia Franceschi (l) and
Deborah Wingert (r), (NYCB, 1986). (Photo by Paul Kolnik)

The return home—
begging my father's
forgiveness . . . (ABT).
(Photo by Martha Swope)

Chapter 15

FOLLOWING my decision to leave ABT, I promised Misha I would still perform the December 1985, Los Angeles season of *Nutcracker*s before I left the company. The company flight to L.A. was scheduled to depart at 5:28 P.M. Even though I knew I had only these last few performances, I had trouble getting myself excited about performing. I packed for the two-week trip in thirty minutes and walked out the door at 4:30 P.M., leaving no time for traffic or any other unforeseen delays in getting to the airport. I immediately put on my Walkman and shut myself off from the world and what I had to do. I checked my watch repeatedly, but thought to myself, When do flights leave on time, anyway?

Watching the seconds ticking away began to bore me and I drifted off in my fantasies. I saw a stage become a football field, green floor, blue backdrop and men lined up in long straight lines waiting for the kickoff—a ballet based on football movements, or maybe basketball, baseball. There were limitless possibilities. By the time the signs for the LaGuardia exits came into view, I knew I had missed the flight.

I was fifteen minutes late. At the ticket counter, I asked if the flight had left. I was told it was departing from the gate as we spoke, but there was another flight to L.A. in three hours.

Better late than never, I thought, and went to get something to eat. Boarding the plane three hours later, I discovered that Danilo Radojevic was on the same flight but no one else from the company. I felt a new sense of independence, traveling on my own. I was no longer a member of anything, a free spirit, no one to hold my hand and make all the arrangements for me.

I used that flight as an exercise in what my life was now going to be like, how I would have to operate, how I would have to take care of all my own business, schedule my time, think about the financial difficulties that would follow. The flight seemed quicker than usual because I was so preoccupied in organizing plans for my future, scheduling my choreographic career, compiling a list of people I would call.

When we arrived in L.A., I made my usual first stop at the car rental office. Normally I rented a compact car, but this time I thought, It's my last season with the company. What the hell? I'll splurge! So I rented a high-priced convertible. In L.A., I usually stayed either with friends or someplace away from the company, but this time I decided to room with Leslie Browne at the Biltmore Hotel, where Charles was also staying.

This season I would be performing the Prince in *The Nutcracker* for the first time. It was a debut and farewell performance all in one. My performances came at the end of the run—one of the three fell on New Year's Eve—and since I had already stopped taking class, I had two weeks to "get it together." My mood was rather peculiar the first day of class. I was blasé, unfocused and indifferent. I wore jazz shoes to ballet class. It was the Christmas season and I concentrated more on buying Christmas presents than on my rehearsals. I wasn't nervous about the debut—I didn't care very much and just wanted to get it over with.

When the time of the performance came, my attitude still hadn't changed. I got to the theatre without leaving time for my usual two-hour preparation of makeup and warming up.

Instead I threw on some pancake and rushed through a short barre. Misha's *Nutcracker* is no easy feat. Unlike other, more conventional *Nutcracker*s, the Prince plays the Nutcracker role in the first act as well.

As the Nutcracker, you have to wear an enormous, heavy mask and two costumes, the Nutcracker's over the Prince's. Feeling very weighted down by the mask and costumes, you have to dance a very demanding solo with quick leaps and turns, while carrying a heavy wooden sword for the duel. Misha created it for himself, so the dancer in the role is challenged to match Misha's kind of power. Feeling that *strength* was the primary characteristic of the role, I put as much punch and athleticism into it as I could without focusing too much on line or technical details.

The Nutcracker mask is braced on your face by spongy pads resting against your cheeks and chin. During dress rehearsal, I noticed that the chin pad in my mask was too big and going into my mouth to the point where I was almost eating it. Before the performance, I tore some of it off, and created a shape that fit more snugly on my chin. I went out and did the Soldiers' Dance, which includes a series of coupé jetés and a duel with the Rat King, after which the Nutcracker falls down in exhaustion. As I fell, I took a deep breath and a piece of the torn sponge went into my mouth and down my throat. Panting there on the floor, I felt the sponge flap in and out of my throat. I thought I was going to choke to death. While attempting to stay in character, I tried desperately to dislodge it from my throat by heaving. I was scared to death. As Drosselmeyer helped me up and lifted the mask from my head to reveal me as the Prince, I took a deep breath of fresh air, exhaled heavily and the sponge flew out of my mouth. It was my first brush with death on stage.

Alessandra Ferri was my Clara. It was very easy dancing the pas de deux with her. She's so small, light and limber. Surprisingly, the performance went very well. I was completely uninhibited. I didn't care what the reviews were going to be like. It was over for me. I was finishing a chapter in my life. There was something about that liberated mental state that helped a lot. It taught me the lesson that when you're finally able to let go of something, you can relax and appreciate it. You know the thrill of freedom!

Then came the second act. This is the technical part for the Prince. Misha didn't construct the conventional pas de deux with adagio, variations and coda. The Prince and Clara dance first in the "Waltz of the Flowers," followed by their variations, the coda and finally the pas de trois with Drosselmeyer. Strengthwise, it's a much better arrangement to get the variation over first, when you're fresh. I wasn't nervous at all. I just went out and danced without caring about details like pointed feet. It was a wonderful experience, probably a first for me in a classical role. For once, I enjoyed being in white tights.

When I finished the variation, I had the feeling I had done a classical variation in the manner it should be approached, shapewise. Usually a variation has three, sometimes four, different sections: the first step, the middle step and the last step. The dancer has to be able to give those sections coloration. Starting from the first step, you must know where to rest and how to approach what follows, how to sustain energy through the jumps and turns and how to save enough to give your all in the ending, and finish well. In terms of energy, I had more often than not been a short-distance runner, starting off with power, then fading out. I learned to do the opposite—start off a little under, then build and build and build.

After the performance, Charles and Misha came backstage to tell me they were very impressed. Charles was especially pleased, thinking I had made great progress. I knew that he was also very disappointed. He still felt it was a mistake for me to leave, and objected to my going through with it. At dinner later that week, Charles tried to convince me one last time to stay with the company at least until the end of the year. He thought I could work out my personal problems and be helping the company at the same time. He pointed out the enormous investment the company had made in my career, and that I owed something to the choreographers who had cast me in three new ballets. To let them down, he felt, would be morally irresponsible. I thought letting *myself* down would be morally irresponsible. He then brought up the issue of the all-Tudor evening, and knowing the respect I felt for Mr. Tudor, he knew I would feel it was the strongest argument for my staying through the year. But it wasn't strong enough.

I didn't want to feel guilty or think I was leaving the company in the lurch. I tried to explain that in my present condition, I wouldn't be much help to the company anyway. If I stayed on and continued the tour, I might do something very destructive. I had never been inclined to be destructive to my own body, but it could happen. I also foresaw the possibility of becoming a disruptive influence in the company, stemming from my resentment over not doing with my life what I really needed to do. I tried to impress upon Charles how very important it was for me to do what I had to do, when I had to do it.

Understandably, it was very upsetting for Charles, not only for professional but for personal reasons as well. Being on those long tours, members of the company, including management, need friends they can relax and feel comfortable with. Charles could relax and feel comfortable with me. I'm not sure how much that aspect influenced his urgency, but it was there and I couldn't let that sway me. For the first time, I felt my self, my life and my opinions were going to be under my own control.

Christmas was especially enjoyable that year. There were lots of parties and presents. Then came my last performance of *Nutcracker* on New Year's Eve, which is always fun but often risky. It was the one performance a year when the dancers did practical jokes, and made up different, usually amusing, choreography and had a good time, almost a *Saturday Night Live* performance of *Nutcracker*.

Misha allowed this after he had come back from his time with the New York City Ballet. NYCB's offbeat New Year's Eve *Nutcracker* has become something of a tradition in New York, and Misha thought it would work in his version. One of the first things he did was to have four different Princes dance with one Clara in the second act. But as time went on, things got a little out of hand, sometimes of questionable taste.

This particular year, one of the Mice made a special guest appearance in "The Waltz of the Snowflakes" scene. There's a point in the dance when the Snowflakes swirl around the stage, then suddenly hit the floor in unison in a "Dying Swan"–type pose. A long trail in the music follows, where choreographically nothing happens. At that moment, roller-skating down the ramp came this half-man/half-rat using snowflakes on sticks as ski poles. It was hysterical.

Harriet Clark, a corps dancer, wore a leopard-skin hat with matching leopard-skin purse and leopard-skin muff with her costume. By the end of the first act party scene, the maid was rip-roaring drunk. There was outlandish makeup and general clowning around. The Chinese dancers came out with take-out Chinese food containers and gave them to the Prince and Clara. When the Shepherd runs off to get the wolf mask to frighten the shepherdess, he came back with a mask of Ronald Reagan. In "The Waltz of the Flowers," where the girls bourée around in an inner circle while the boys waltz around in and out, they reversed roles. Instead of the usual group pose at the end of "The Waltz of the Flowers," the dancers ran offstage leaving Clara and the Prince alone.

I suggested to Alex Ferri that she make her entrance with the candle in Act I as the Sleepwalker from Balanchine's *La Sonnambula,* and that when she got to the Nutcracker, to step over it. The only thing I did as the Prince was at the end of the Snowflake scene. The Prince pushes Clara around on a sleigh, she twirls around, he lifts her and together they run up the ramp as the curtain falls. Instead, I pushed the sleigh downstage right, helped her out, and we walked slowly center stage and then straight up stage as they do at the Act I finale of Balanchine's *Nutcracker.*

Misha was out of town, but heard what had gone on. This time he sent a message that from then on, the performance would be done straight without any more clowning around. There were even rumors of dancers being fired. But I don't think the dancers were too concerned. They needed their one day of fun.

Looking back, it was ironic that I made two allusions to Balanchine ballets in that New Year's Eve performance, not knowing, never dreaming, that one day I would be in his former company.

At my last performance, I received tons of flowers, including a wreath from Nora Kaye and Herb Ross whose kindness and support gave me additional strength to do what I felt I needed to do, and lots of letters saying how I would be missed, with hopes that I would come back. It didn't feel like an ending. It wasn't a sad occasion, like being forced by old age into retirement. It was a beginning, which was only underscored by the fact that it was all happening on New Year's Eve.

All the allusions to my "coming back" struck me as odd, because what I was going through had to do with moving forward, not leaving temporarily, with intentions of going back. I had made a major life-changing decision that wasn't simply an emotional reaction to a hard time. Having recognized that during my sessions with Laurel Morris, I felt I had gotten the help I needed from her, and planned not to continue when I returned to New York. So, I wasn't very sentimental about this "farewell," although it was very touching. As a member of ABT, I had had wonderful experiences, wonderful memories of having been touched through my work with incredible artists. But I wanted to go on and find more.

Eight years is a long time in a twenty-six-year-old dancer's life. A chapter was finished and it was time to turn the page. The aim of my life was to start over, and I found it relatively easy to come back to New York for a new beginning. I got a new calendar datebook, with all the pages clean, and anticipated filling them up with plans based on fresh ideas. Admittedly it was a little scary. I wasn't completely finished with ABT—they would be back in New York for a rehearsal period, and I had agreed to help teach my parts in the new ballets for the upcoming season: Karole Armitage's *Mollino Room*, MacMillan's *Requiem*, and David Gordon's *Murder*.

I didn't take class. I would wake up in the morning and spend two hours over coffee and the New York *Times*. I listened to music, got ideas for choreography and made lots of phone calls. Then I'd go to the studio. I felt I could breathe easier and feel relaxed around the company. I felt under my own control. Many of the dancers still didn't believe that I was actually not going to be there on a regular basis. It was hard for them to believe because they hadn't seen any visible reasons for why I would leave. There was no one to blame, no situation to pinpoint.

The dance public also seemed to find my leaving ABT difficult to understand. Soon after my return to New York, I had calls from several papers for interviews. I ignored the requests, feeling no need to explain myself to the press. I did approve a press release in New York before I left for the L.A. season. It was very general, announcing that Mikhail Baryshnikov regretted that Robert La Fosse would be leaving American Ballet Theatre to pursue other interests, etc. I half expected the New York *Post* and the New York *Times* at least to investigate the reasons behind my leaving. To my knowledge, they never responded to the release. I can only assume that some writers wanted to leave the reasons open for speculation, as an addition to their stockpile of ammunition against Misha. No one knew *why* I had left; they could only speculate. My suspicions were confirmed by an article that came out around that time, discussing the dancers Misha had lost, including Fernando and myself, and wondering what Misha was doing to cause these "defections." They offered no real reasons for why either Fernando and I left, simply assuming that somehow it was Misha's fault. It wasn't only unfair and cruel, it was bad reporting. As a result, rumors flew. Most said I had had a fight with Misha. It was ridiculous, pointless and it hurt people, including Misha. But I suppose what counts to some people is a good story.

In December, I had started singing lessons with my friend Kenneth's voice teacher, Patty Allison. Patty is a fantastic woman, a member of the New York City Opera, with an incredible soprano voice. A cute, pudgy blond, she has a distinctive teaching method that utilizes some pretty crass images. Wanting a singer to breathe properly by pushing air out with the diaphragm, she'd say, "Fart that note" or "Sing from the balls." She'd demonstrate rapid breathing by placing one of my hands on her stomach, the other on her back, then she'd pant like a dog. She could expand her stomach and lower back in and out like an inflatable beach ball. Even her rump vibrated. After so many years of dancing, my butt was entirely too tight ever to get the same effect.

Patty had limitless energy. She was also into yoga. Sometimes she'd make me lie on the floor on a roller to relax while I sang. I could relate to her physical approach. She loved the challenge of working with dancers, because they're often very tense and can't breathe. She talked a lot and sang along with me. She told me how exciting it would be for her to train an outstanding dancer to sing an aria. She gave me great encouragement and her sheer excitement inspired me. She was like a singing analyst for me at the time. I needed that kind of support.

When I got back from L.A. on January 3, 1986, Jerome Robbins called me and invited me to join the New York City Ballet. After the initial shock, my response was to respectfully refuse, not feeling able to join one major ballet company so soon after leaving another. I told Jerry I wanted to be on my own, primarily to choreograph. He understood, but told me to think about it anyway.

Following the rehearsal period with ABT, I went back to Beaumont to choreograph a group ballet for Marsha Woody's advanced students. I wanted to use this opportunity more as a choreographic experiment than as the making of a performance piece. I wanted to try different choreographic patterns out on eight dancers. I used the Tchaikovsky Third Symphony, the music Balanchine used for the "Diamonds" section of his ballet *Jewels*. I wasn't too pleased with the results. The dancers were very young, in their early teens, and with the exception of one girl, hadn't yet achieved a professional level of working. It was hard for me. I was used to working with professional dancers, not thirteen- and fourteen-year-olds. At times I felt I was working with hardened clay. But I finished the piece, *Cambiare* ("To Change"), showed it and received a courteous response.

While I was in Texas, I wrote Jerry Robbins a letter explaining that I considered his offer to join NYCB an honor and hadn't meant to sound ungrateful. I thanked him very much and said I would give it some more thought, but at the moment I had no idea what I really wanted to do. I added that perhaps sometime in the future he would ask again and I would readily accept.

Discouraged with my ballet, I took the first available flight from Texas to New York. I did a great deal of thinking on that flight and realized for the first time that I was now really on my own. My first independent effort wasn't a disaster, but I didn't have the security of American Ballet Theatre to fall back on. I couldn't hide, get lost in the shuffle in a company of one hundred dancers.

I had no idea what I would do next. There was the possibility of returning to Broadway. My agents, Mary Day and David Roos, had been busy negotiating for me to star as the dancing lead in *Song and Dance*. The producers knew my work, were interested and wanted to know my schedule. I wasn't sure if I really wanted to commit myself. I thought Bernadette Peters was sensational in the show and would have loved to work with her. But I didn't see it as a great step forward in my career. Choreographer Peter Martins had tailor-made the dancing lead for Christopher d'Amboise, and I wanted to make it clear that if I *did* do the show, I would like Peter to adapt it for me. I wanted to work with the choreographer. I didn't want to be just plugged into the part.

I had meetings with several people involved with *Song and Dance*, including Peter Martins, who was also co-Ballet Master in Chief with Jerry Robbins of New York City Ballet. I went to the New York State Theater to meet with him before a New York City Ballet performance. I found it fairly amusing that although I had worked next door at the Metropolitan Opera House at Lincoln Center my entire career, I was a fish out of water backstage at the New York State Theatre and got lost.

Peter was a real gentleman. In that deep Danish voice of his, he offered me a glass of wine and made me feel very comfortable. He said, "I hear you want to do *Song and Dance*. Why? What are you doing now?"

"Well, Peter," I said frankly, "if I do a show like *Song and Dance*, I will have time during the day to work on my choreography, get a few projects going, maybe do some workshops." He thought it was a great idea and started to figure out some dates.

213

As I got up to leave the meeting, Peter said, "Of course, after you do *Song and Dance,* you'll come and join the New York City Ballet, yes?"

"Well, Peter," I said, smiling, "we'll burn that bridge when we come to it. I mean, we'll come to that bridge when we cross it. I mean . . . oh, you know what I mean!"

Shortly after that, I called Jerry and said I wanted to have lunch. We met for lunch at a restaurant across the street from the New York State Theater and I told him that I might be doing *Song and Dance.* He suggested that I might get bored doing the same show night after night, and besides, I had other career options. I explained to him that I really didn't want to work in a situation where I had to devote a lot of time, because I wanted to concentrate on my choreography and other projects like singing lessons. I felt that doing a Broadway show would enable me to do that.

In the meantime, I would audition for a few television commercials, including one for Bounce, choreographed by Louis Falco. Ironically, a lot of kids from *Song and Dance* auditioned, too. It would be good money. Remembering that I made the same amount of money for one Dr. Pepper commercial that I made in an entire year in the corps at ABT, I knew I could probably continue to make a lot of money that way, leaving me time for the projects I had planned.

Jerry appreciated my situation, but said he had to know my answer by the end of the week. He was doing a new ballet for the spring season and had to know what dancers he would have to work with. There was a special urgency to his need. In the interim between Jerry's first call to me in January and the present meeting, Joseph Duell, an outstanding and versatile young principal dancer with the company, had tragically committed suicide. I told Jerry I understood the pressure, but would still have to sleep on it.

As I thought about it more and more, I realized the opportunity to dance with the New York City Ballet might never come again. But I was afraid that joining NYCB so soon after leaving ABT might not look right to Misha. I didn't want him to resent me for making the step. On the other hand, Misha wasn't my father after all, and I was no longer on salary. It wasn't that I didn't owe him anything, but I knew that I had worked hard and earned what I had done in my career. I reasoned that he himself had left ABT for NYCB and would probably understand.

I called Misha to tell him what I was thinking. He said he thought my joining New York City Ballet was a great idea and felt I would fit in very well. He also offered some advice. "They go very fast there and you can easily get lost," he warned. "They have so many ballets in their repertoire and they work so quickly, you have to take very good care of yourself. Stay in class, don't get too relaxed and use a lot of self-discipline."

The next day, I was scheduled to work as a choreographer on a hair-shampoo commercial. Perhaps one of the reasons choreography became so interesting to me was because I could see what I was doing. The hardest thing for me as a choreographer is to be actually objective about a dance after I've made it. I can look at other people's choreography and know what I would have done to that music. But I can't look at my own choreography and judge whether it uses the stage well enough, if it fits the music or how it feels to me. I can't step away yet and feel what an audience would feel. In the beginning it was because I danced in my own ballets, such as *Rappaccini's Daughter*, but I've never been completely happy with anything I've choreographed. That will change, I hope, with time.

My first choreography to be shown professionally in New York was for the AIDS benefit at the Metropolitan Opera House on Sunday, November 3, 1985.

I heard about plans for the benefit and immediately wanted to be a part of the program. I called the producers Barry

Brown and the late Fritz Holt, and asked if I could perform. They were very pleased to have the New York premiere of *Rappaccini's Daughter*, which I had danced with Leslie Browne on programs with Misha's touring company.

Since he and Robert Lord had originally given me the idea for the ballet, Gary Lisz was thrilled that I had actually choreographed some of it and that it would be on the AIDS benefit program. During one of our rehearsals, Gary walked in late. Leslie and I were rehearsing with Elaine Kudo and John Gardner. Never having seen the ballet, he didn't know what to expect. What he saw was two couples dancing exactly the same steps, one couple in front, one behind.

He rushed up to me the second we finished and there were almost tears in his eyes. "Oh, Robby! How did you ever come up with that *wild* double mirror image? It's *brilliant!*"

"Gary," I said, slightly embarrassed, "they're not *in* the ballet. They're the second cast."

The word got out that Misha, who had been out of town finishing *White Nights*, would be back and had decided to be on the program. He had been asked before, but wouldn't commit himself at first. Peter Fonseca had also choreographed a ballet for Misha's tour. His ballet usually started the program. It was based on a ballet class, starting at the barre, moving to the center and ending with Misha doing incredible turns and jumps. When Misha decided he would do the benefit, he said he wanted to dance Peter's ballet.

The benefit program was getting very long, and now with Misha participating, the producers called and asked me if I would cut two or three minutes from the pas de deux. I told them there really wasn't any way I could do that and retain the integrity of the piece, but if they wanted to cut the pas de deux altogether, I would understand. They didn't like that option, so Leslie and I were scheduled.

It was one of the most moving and inspiring evenings of my life. The program included an impressive array of performers and celebrities—Bette Midler, Christopher Reeve, Chita Rivera, Carol Burnett, Dorothy Loudon, Colleen Dewhurst, the Gay Men's Chorus—and I felt very moved by their appreciation of our dancing and proud to be part of this bold statement by the artistic community in support of its friends and colleagues.

But the most memorable moment of all was left to Bette Midler. She sashayed out on the stage of the Metropolitan Opera House as if she had just hopped into a pair of shoes that were already moving on their own. There she stood, luscious breasts and all, and started out by asking the gala audience if they ever thought they'd live to see the day that they heard anyone from the stage of the Met say "FUCK!" The usual raucous stuff. Then slowly, almost imperceptibly, she altered the tone. She reminisced about her start at the Continental Baths and her early days of living above piano bars on Grove Street. She remembered the happy singing voices she heard coming from below. "How many of those voices from those days come back to me," she told us. "And how many of them are with us here tonight?" Her words evoked a mental image of slowly diminishing voices, slowly fading songs.

"This is a war," she continued. "We're soldiers, and we've got to fight. We can't let this happen. We've got to fight!"

By this time, there were enough tears in that audience to fill an ocean. As she sang "The Rose" and closed with a heart-rending "I'll Be Seeing You," every eye in the house, from the audience to the performers peering out from the wings, was riveted on the Divine Miss M.

But if the AIDS benefit was one of my best experiences with choreography, not to mention raising money for a desperately deserving cause, being the choreographer on the shampoo commercial was a horrendous experience. The director was an obnoxious egomaniac. I had choreographed an entire dance to

217

the commercial's music, but he only wanted a lot of jumping and asked, "Do you think that girl can do *ten* pirouettes, you know, just keep *spinning*?"

"Of course not," I answered back, not too respectfully. "Only Cynthia Gregory, on a good day, could do that. And this girl is definitely *not* Cynthia Gregory. She was obviously chosen for her hair and her beauty, not for her ability to dance." People from the agency were there with the commercial clients who had selected this girl. Here I was, telling the director that the girl they had chosen was not technically up to the part. I later heard that the clients felt I was bad-mouthing their choice of talent.

Unfortunately, what I said was the truth. They had absolutely no idea of what a ballet dancer is capable of doing. Furthermore, they had her dressed, complete with leg-warmers, in an outfit they imagined a ballet dancer in a working situation would wear. I had never seen anything like it.

The director became very upset and made me feel that *I* was being difficult. What they finally used in the commercial had none of my original choreography. It was simply this girl with beautiful hair just jumping around. At one point I gave up, sat down and watched the rest of the shoot without offering any advice. My decision was almost made for me. If this was what life in the "outside world" was going to be like, I would definitely accept Jerry's offer.

I was never really exposed to New York City Ballet when I was young. I had only seen *The Nutcracker* on television with George Balanchine as Drosselmeyer. When I came to New York each summer, I usually went to ABT because I was overwhelmed by all the stars and the theatricality of the ballets. When I did go to see NYCB, I didn't see any of the great pieces. I didn't see *Serenade* or *Symphony in C*; I saw very strange programs. I thought the corps de ballet was always very messy and I wasn't used to their style. I didn't understand it and didn't like it. I suppose it had a lot to do with my training. I got it into my head that I wanted to join ABT, although a lot of my friends in New York thought I would be more suited to the Balanchine style. I never understood why.

I wanted to dance more than anything, but I also had wanted to be "a star." At NYCB there weren't stars in the conventional sense. There was the company and the stars were made through Mr. Balanchine's choreography. You went to see the New York City Ballet dance the works of Balanchine and Jerome Robbins. NYCB star dancers weren't "hyped," their promotion was very low profile. Casting wasn't announced in the newspapers. It was posted in the New York State Theater lobby a week in advance. ABT promoted its stars by announcing who would be dancing weeks in advance to boost ticket sales. Since I had wanted to make "a name" in the dance world, ABT was where I planned to do it.

I never thought much about Balanchine or NYCB until I actually danced *Prodigal Son*. When I saw *Prodigal Son* during one of my summers in New York, I wasn't that impressed, because there wasn't much of what I considered "dancing" in it. But I'll always remember Edward Villella in that very last crawl at the end of the ballet. To me it was and is one of the most touching moments in ballet; so simple, yet so effective. It brought tears to my eyes.

Oddly enough, Edmund had danced the Prodigal in the National Ballet of Washington production and had a great success in it. But I never imagined myself as the Prodigal Son. It wasn't a role that I related to or felt anything for in my personal life or as a young dancer. Therefore I had never wanted to dance that part or any of the ballets at NYCB. NYCB is a company for women, I thought at the time, and I can understand why a *woman* would want to dance there; the repertoire is for *them*.

So, it wasn't until I performed Balanchine's *Prodigal* and *Symphonie Concertante* at ABT that I began to realize that his ballets contained so much that I missed entirely as a young dancer. I started going to the New York City Ballet whenever I could, sometimes two or three times a week. Seeing more of the repertoire, I began to understand and like the way the dancers danced and see that men indeed played a very large part in his work.

Everyone in NYCB danced "bigger" than we did at ABT. They had more energy. They didn't have the placement of the ABT dancers, but I could see how to the untrained eye it would seem more exciting than the more controlled style of ABT's corps.

I began to read about Balanchine and his theories and like nearly everyone else in the dance world became fascinated with Balanchine, his ballets, the way he ran a company, the way he treated people. I started to think, Boy, I would like to dance with New York City Ballet. I never thought it would be possible because I had always heard that, with few exceptions, they didn't take people into the company unless they came in directly from the School of American Ballet, NYCB's official school, and I had only studied there one summer. Even if I had thought it possible at the time, it would have been a very scary thing to make such a change. It would have been like moving away from home or any other traumatic change. Until it hit me right between the eyes, I never seriously considered moving from American Ballet Theatre to New York City Ballet.

Jerry Robbins left New York for the country two days after our lunch. When I called, he had already gone. I had no way of telling him I was accepting his offer to join the company until the day before I started work.

Chapter 16

ONE of the reasons I left ABT was my not being able to pay the proper amount of attention to my friends in New York. I had a whole set of friends outside the ballet who I didn't get to see for the four or five months out of the year that we toured. You begin to weigh things as you get older and sometimes, I feel, friends become more important than your career.

A dancer's life is hard. I would like to take someone in a more conventional job and make him follow me through my schedule for a week. As I took class, he would have to do aerobics, something physical, and continue doing that as I rehearsed. He could rest when I rested, but he'd move when I moved. He'd eat what I eat, come to the theatre and put makeup on and aerobicize when I was onstage. Do everything with me for a week to see what it's like.

Dancers start their careers at a very young age, and like anything that you start when you're young, what you do becomes second nature. You no longer think about what it takes. You start off taking one class a day as a child. As a teenager, you take more. You start building. You join a company and start rehearsing five or six hours a day, then perform. You start to live it. You never stop to think that this is crazy. You go all day long, and because you go all day long, you spend an inordinate amount of time with yourself and you learn a lot about yourself, especially from the mirror. I never liked my feet or legs in the mirror. When you look at another dancer's legs that make a better shape or line in the mirror, that's all you can think of.

Most people walk around unconscious of their bodies, but dancers spend their whole day looking at the shape of their body, examining it like scientists examining a specimen under a microscope. That's all we focus on. A dancer can become obsessed with how the arches of his feet curve. Is a woman standing behind a counter at Saks concerned about her arches? At the most, she only cares if she can pinch an inch. It's bizarre how intense dancers get with their physicality. They can become obsessed with what they consider their imperfections and often overlook their attributes.

The mirror can bring out imperfections. Dancers can get mesmerized by what they see in the mirror. One of the wonderful things about working with Jerry Robbins is that in rehearsal he has the dancers face away from the mirror. You're not allowed to look at it. He wants the dancers' focus to be where it's needed in performance. He wants us to dance with each other, to make eye contact, really *look* at each other. I often wonder what would happen to dancers if mirrors were banned from ballet studios. Dancers have gotten to use the mirror as a crutch, relying on it as their eye, rather than trusting the person running the rehearsal. As a dancer, you must be able to rely on the objective opinion of the ballet-master. Your opinion cannot be objective about yourself.

The element of performing that has always confused me is not the *feeling* of what you're giving, but the inability to *see* it. Much of my relationship with Charles was based on his being someone who could be objective about my dancing and feel free to make constructive criticisms. It got to the point where he could say everything to me. Every night after performance, we would inevitably discuss what I did, from technical niceties to the way I approached the shape of a variation, to the degree of security I displayed on stage. Dancers are very insecure that way. They work in total isolation from the audience. They never *see* what they do. They're always giving, giving, giving.

People often ask dancers how they remember so many different steps in so many ballets. My answer has always been that it's the same process by which people remember foreign languages or poems, lines in a play or trivia. How do people remember trivia? It's something they exercise within themselves. A dancer's ability to remember choreography is extraordinary to some people. I'm fascinated by people who can use their mind and their voice and their memory.

Dancers spend their lives in a studio with music and other people telling them what to do. They're basically nonverbal. They say very little. It's a silent process. They use their bodies, their eyes, their ears, but they rarely use their speech in the work process. They don't have to talk. Dancers become extremely disciplined and receptive in a silent world. So there's frustration when you come out of the theatre wanting to exercise the brain in areas outside of music and dance steps. We're asked to be seen and not heard, like my father always used to say.

When dancers have a chance to speak, they most often speak in visual associations and images, because dance is imagery. When a dancer gets to the point where he can comfortably express himself verbally, it's extraordinary. When they finally get a chance to talk, dancers often start foaming at the mouth; they erupt like a volcano and it's hard to stop them.

As a choreographer for example I need a concept, an idea or strong visual images to be able to choreograph. I can't approach the creation of a dance as something abstract, as dance for dance's sake. I've never easily understood the abstract. I don't understand throwing paint on a canvas. I have come to appreciate, even like, a certain abstraction in art, like Klee or Miró, for color and emotional tension. But for myself in choreography, I have to have a starting point, somewhere to come from and someplace to go to.

I've learned a lot from my new work as a choreographer. I see how young dancers become tools, instruments waiting for their next command. But I've learned how dancers can contribute to the creative process. There are times when dancers might not understand exactly what the choreographer wants and do something else instead. Sometimes that's just as good or better. Dancers can actually help the choreographic process. I always felt as a dancer that I would like to have some degree of input with the choreographer. I suppose most choreographers would resist that, because they want to be in control, which at its worst can become a power trip. On the other hand it can be irritating for a choreographer not to start to work on a clean slate. I now know the need for freedom to put all the pieces together without resistance.

But I also need the input of the dancers. I encourage that, or at least try to encourage that. I frequently say, "Do what *you* would do. Do something that I wouldn't think of." Some dancers respond immediately to that approach and feel where the piece is going. Others can't. The ones who connect with a choreographer are the ones who can best be choreographed on, and a dancer can have a very reliable, even outstanding career that way. Without even knowing that much about it, I suspect that Suzanne Farrell's career was like that. She did what she was told, but she also brought a great deal of her own consciousness and dance intelligence to what was going on at the time. She didn't do steps literally. She interpreted the movement the way she thought the choreographer would want it. I feel that when I see her dance. You feel that the choreography is something coming from within her, not something that was put on her.

There is that element in dance that even though you are

dancing someone else's choreography, you have to make it look to the audience like your own or that of the character you're dancing. Learning these things has helped my dancing. I've learned to be in more control of myself on stage, to dance with more power. To give a good performance, I've had to learn that *I'm* the one who's up there, and if I fall one way, I have to go with it and not force myself to stay within the confines of the choreography and risk sacrificing the performance. Regardless of whether you're on track with the choreography, you have to deliver a performance of a certain level. You have to deliver the best, not of what *should* be, but the best of what is going to happen at the moment. That's what great dancers like Suzanne Farrell do. They go with what's happening that night. If they're "on" for a pirouette, they go for it. If they're off, they do something else, or if they feel they're going to fall, they fall that way. They don't just fall down. They make everything appear like it's what they *wanted* to do.

Sometimes you work with choreographers who want such a specific thing that you'll never achieve it if you're working only for that. Jerry Robbins, for example, wants a very specific thing. He's very detailed and fine-lined about the way he wants his steps done. But I never have felt that way with his choreography.

Many dancers try so hard to do exactly what Jerry wants stylistically, they get in a bind. Jerry's choreography is influenced by many sources, his Russian-Judaic background, ballet, Broadway, jazz. He uses a lot of classical steps, but they're very deliberate, having a forceful contact with the floor, and a definite sense of movement, almost *pushing* through space. You have to be very conscious of weight distribution to dance his ballets. Some dancers try to duplicate exactly what they achieved in rehearsal rather than bending with or accepting whatever happens onstage in order to achieve some kind of *performance*. Of course you have to be on the right count and do the arms Jerry asks for in the choreography, but when you're on stage, that's the *real* moment. It's not a rehearsal where you can stop and do it over. If you mess up, you can't let the audience know that. You have to be professional enough to cover up.

Some dancers try to imitate what Jerry wants, because Jerry is such a great dancer. He still shows all of his movements, he can show the body, the torso, the posture and the weight. He can show so much. I've found that when I try to imitate him, it works against me. I have to express what he's saying or feeling through my own physical terms. If it doesn't work, you try something different. You adapt. You don't get your eye set on a certain picture and try to duplicate that picture. You take from that picture, that movement, an idea, an expression or a feeling that he's going for, and put that feeling inside of your body and it will come out. You work from in to out, not from out to in. You don't plaster choreography on your body. You don't imitate something and make the emotions from that. It's the emotion that brings out the physical.

Agnes de Mille was like Jerome Robbins in that she wanted her movement done in a very specific manner, because it was very stylized. Bob Fosse is another specifically stylized choreographer with the hip cocked and the hand spread open and the shoulders cocked, the head down, the bopping of the knees or the feet—the kind of movement you didn't learn in your everyday tap, jazz or ballet class.

Twyla Tharp is very exact about where she wants the positions, with a little bit of looseness. You have more leeway with Twyla. She gives you "X" number of steps to do within "Y" counts of music. She makes a ballet on *you*. Dancers sometimes struggle to do the steps because they're so hard. There's a constant shifting of weight. She never remembers her own choreography. She does it and it's gone from her brain. She knows how bodies should move in her choreography, but Jerry remembers every step and can usually do every role in his ballets, the way Misha could.

Misha could do every one of those character roles in *Don Quixote*. That was one of the most extraordinary things about those rehearsals. He could get up and do Sancho Panza, Don Q, Basil, Kitri, Gamache, the Toreador, because he had to show everybody who the characters were and what they were expressing. It was fascinating to watch him switch back and forth from one to the other, and then to see the dancers do their imitations of what he had done. He was a one-man gallery of character studies.

Remembering those *Don Q* rehearsals at the outset of my career, I can't help reflecting on the inside view I had of the major transition I saw at American Ballet Theatre during my years there; a transition due to the artistic vision of Mikhail Baryshnikov.

Misha did things very quickly at ABT, changing the company in many ways. When we moved to 890 Broadway, for example, we suddenly had seven studios to work in; the cumbersome method of scheduling rehearsals was revamped and computerized; character classes were started to train dancers in the tradition of classical mime, something that was sorely lacking in classics like *Swan Lake* and *Giselle*. But most important was Misha's unquestionable desire to develop talent from within the company, which had been largely ignored before.

The technique of ABT's corps had never been one of the company's strongest assets; audiences came to see ABT for its stars. I think Misha, with the help of Georgina Parkinson, Elena Tchernichova, and the rest of the faculty, has stressed the importance of a good, solid technical foundation. Today, the ABT corps has never looked stronger, with many talented soloists and principals on the rise. Misha and his staff gambled on a long-term investment. What Lucia did was very different. She approached ABT in terms of box office. She wanted to sell tickets, and so she imported an array of international stars, while the "rank and file" suffered from benign neglect. When I joined ABT, the soloist level was nowhere near the level of principal dancers, and the corps de ballet was not very far from the soloists in technical ability. Instead of being encouraged to concentrate on developing a firm technical and stylistic foundation, the ABT corps de ballet, the products of many different schools and teaching methods all over America, had to spend hours in a rehearsal room just coping with the demands of the gamut of choreographic styles and preparing to back up guest artists.

When a new director takes over a company it takes at least five years before it has any real effect. It takes another five years for it to blossom. Misha's artistic policy has made sense. You make an investment in your product, allow time for it to develop, and watch it grow stronger. It has a lot to do with trust. Dancers must believe that someone has faith in them.

Part III

NEW YORK CITY BALLET

Chapter 17

THERE I was in tights again. It was March 11, 1986, my first day with the New York City Ballet. I hadn't been nervous for a class since my audition for ABT almost ten years before. In fact, it was worse. I was an adult now, a former principal dancer with NYCB's "rival company." I was nervous when I walked into the New York State Theater and into a room full of relative strangers. Adding to my uneasiness was knowing that since the decision had been made so quickly, no one knew exactly why I was there. At first, most of them assumed I was only there to take class, but I'm sure there were those who figured it out rather quickly. I already had a few friends in the company, and they asked me what I was doing there. All I could answer was "Well, I work here now." Fortunately, they seemed to be excited about it.

I looked around the class and saw these extraordinary dancers. Patricia McBride, Suzanne Farrell, Kyra Nichols, Maria Calegari, Sean Lavery, Ib Anderson. I couldn't keep my eyes off Suzanne Farrell. She was like a porcelain figure. From where she stood, the arrangement of the barres made it appear that the whole company was watching her. Since they had just come back from a layoff, the dancers were pretty out of shape. I was in relatively good shape, so I didn't look so bad. I did a pretty good class. Actually I felt it was a *really* good class. I was performing, naturally.

Violette Verdy, who was teaching, came over to me. "Are you with us now?" she greeted me in her fluttering half-French/half-English. When I answered that I was, she seemed delighted and, like a cheerful zephyr, breezed away to begin class.

Because this was a class for the Balanchine company, everything was executed much quicker than I was used to. But my nerves and the situation made me ready for it. The tendus, for example, were done so quickly that I couldn't keep up. It takes a while to build up that kind of speed. It's like running or jogging; you've just got to keep doing it to build up your stamina in order to get faster and faster. That's what any kind of physical training is all about.

I had a rehearsal the very first day of the rehearsal period, which is rather unusual for NYCB principal dancers. Jerry was starting a new ballet to Aaron Copland music called "Quiet City," which Copland had written for a play. For the rehearsal, Jerry used a recording of the music and also a pianist. Peter Boal and Damian Woetzel were called to rehearsal along with me, but I didn't know whether they were understudies or actually a part of the ballet. He started out with them, so I knew there were three of us.

He had them come on one at a time from the corner and do very godlike movements. At a certain point in the music trumpets called out, and he told me to run, jump and fly in the air as they lifted me even higher. At the moment, I thought this was going to be Jerome Robbins' version of *Apollo*. From the first step, I felt this was a ballet about the heavens, something spiritual. I understood what he was after, even though Jerry doesn't ever really say what he's doing. Sometimes he doesn't know exactly what he's going for, but he has the seed of an idea that develops as he's doing it.

It went very quickly and other dancers in the company were amazed, because he's usually noted for doing something, then changing it, then changing it again and winding up with a Version A and Version B, and you're supposed to remember each version. He also has a reputation for being very difficult and in this experience, none of that proved true. He created the movement very quickly. He knew exactly what he wanted.

At one point during the week, he brought in a big group of corps de ballet dancers. He started out with them scattered all over the stage, looking different ways and listening. At one point they separated and that's where the three of us came in. He did the corps rehearsals separately. He had them sitting on the stage to watch our section and then, at one point, get up and dance themselves. He did that for about two days, and then we never saw that version again. Clearly, he went from one conception to a completely different one in a matter of two days. In the final version, the corps never danced.

He completed the ballet in two weeks. I was really knocking myself out for Jerry, although he told me to take it easy, not to do everything "full-out." But it didn't matter. I was going to do everything full-out, because I had the desire to prove myself all over again. I was working with someone whose work I respected so much, it didn't matter if I knocked myself out.

This happens when dancers truly appreciate a choreographer. You're willing to give whatever you need to give. Choreographers really respond to dancers who will try almost anything. The dancers are the choreographer's instruments, their paintbrushes; they are also their medium, their clay. The choreographer must be able to mold them. If you don't have that understanding as a dancer, if you say, "I can't do that, that's not possible," instead of allowing yourself the imagination to think maybe it *is* possible, or perhaps it can be done

233

another way or if you don't allow yourself to be totally vulnerable, the choreographer won't be able to make that experience or idea a reality.

That's one of the reasons I feel comfortable working with new choreographers. I allow myself to be vulnerable. Some dancers are simply not choreographer's dancers. They can't be easily choreographed on. They're limiting themselves for some reason. But I never had that problem. I find it true in life as well. If you don't open yourself to others, you cut yourself off from developing potential friendships.

Jerry was also working on another new ballet. I think it was the third version or so of Stravinsky's "Dumbarton Oaks." He had done a little bit of it with Maria Calegari and Joe Duell and they had it on videotape. I was called to rehearsal with Maria, Darci Kistler, Peter Frame and David Otto. They turned on the tape machine and there was Joe Duell. I can't imagine what those dancers who had known and worked with him for many years must have been feeling. I know I felt terribly uncomfortable, and I had only known him through his dancing on stage and had had lunch with him once.

Those rehearsals were difficult for Jerry and the others learning it off the tape. He kept changing the section he had started for Joe and Maria, the opening of the second movement. The counts were all very different. At one point, Jerry felt I had too much to learn, and that "Dumbarton Oaks" wasn't important enough for me to spend time learning at that point. I understood what he was saying, but I came back the next day and told him that I didn't care how much of a work load I had. I wanted to do that ballet, because I wanted to work with him as much as possible. I had heard that Jerry will often make a ballet for someone and then change the casting at the last minute, and I didn't want that to happen.

As we rehearsed it, we played "change your partners." I did it with Darci, then I did it with Maria. David did it. Peter did it. Jerry kept switching people around. As the ballet developed, it started to look rather "cute." I had never seen his earlier versions, so I didn't know what Jerry really wanted from it. Finally, when we had our costume fittings, I saw they had a commedia dell'arte style to them. So, it wasn't until I saw the costumes that I understood how to dance it. When it was completed, Darci and I were cast in the principal roles.

Darci is one dancer at NYCB who I especially feel has a great deal to offer me personally. I admire her warmth, her great talent and her intelligence. When I used to watch NYCB performances in the last five or six years, I used to fantasize about dancing with her. Before the premiere of *Piccolo Balleto*, the new Stravinsky ballet, I danced with Darci in *Prodigal Son*.

NYCB was reviving *Prodigal Son* that season. I had heard they were reviving it for Ib Andersen, but I was naturally happy to be called to rehearsals, too. The ballet had been out of the repertoire for some time, and Rosemary Dunleavy, the ballet mistress, didn't really know it because formerly it had been John Taras' ballet to stage and John was now at ABT.

We began working from a tape of Misha dancing *Prodigal* for the PBS "Dance in America" series. Watching that tape, I remembered Misha telling me that since that version was mounted for television Mr. Balanchine had restaged things for the particular needs of the television camera. So many of the things on that tape were not in the stage version that John had set at ABT. They often asked my opinion, but I didn't want to be put in that situation. I was in this company to learn their *Prodigal Son*. It was a new experience, and I didn't want to be called upon to recreate what I had done at ABT. I didn't want to be at the center of any ABT/NYCB "disputes." So, more times than not, my memory "failed"—I just didn't remember—and I went along with the way they were setting it.

I learned something at ABT. Natasha Makarova once said that when you're working in the studio with other dancers, you have to help each other and do it willingly. But it's always good not to tell them *all* your "secrets." I went through the rehearsals knowing that when I finally went out on stage, I would bring all my former experience in the role to my performance.

The moment came in those rehearsals when I had to partner Suzanne Farrell. I wasn't quite ready to touch Suzanne Farrell. I didn't want to chance breaking that "delicate porcelain figurine." We came to the point where I put my head between her legs, lift her up on my shoulders and let her slide down my back. As she slid down my back, I realized this was one of the *strongest* women I had ever partnered! The amount of control she demonstrated in that moment was a revelation. Grabbing hold of me, she wasn't the least bit delicate. Her dancing was strong and deliberate, not at all what her lyrical physicality leads you to believe. I was rather nervous to dance with her. She's very shy. Nevertheless, it was the single most gratifying moment I'd had thus far at NYCB.

As the rehearsal period went on, Kyra Nichols, the ballerina I was originally cast with in *Prodigal,* was taken out because her work load was so heavy. I was cast with Darci. In our first rehearsals, I felt that Darci was not really a siren. She's certainly beautiful, but she's more on the sweet-sixteen side. The Siren in *Prodigal Son* should be a woman of awesome beauty who, even as she stands there, compels you to have sex with her. Since it's not in Darci's nature to openly project that kind of image, she was slower than the rest at learning the part. I sensed that taking on the Siren would be a difficult task for her. Fortunately, Darci is the kind of dancer who likes to use rehearsals to figure things out.

Those rehearsals were the beginning of a very exciting partnership for me. I had finally found someone I felt especially comfortable in the rehearsal room with, a dancer I felt was on my same level. I was willing to go through whatever it took to help her and she knew it. In those rehearsals, she frequently remembered things that Mr. Balanchine had said. He often cast dancers against type as a challenge and exercise in artistic growth, and Darci believed in this. Darci's only frame of reference for the role of the Siren was what she had seen Karin von Aroldingen and Suzanne do in performance. She didn't want to be derivative, and struggled to find an original interpretation. I felt Darci needed to find what it was about herself that could help her interpretation—even things like the way she tilts her head or holds her neck, her posture, the weight and deliberateness she can give certain movements.

During one rehearsal, we got to the part in the pas de deux where she has to sit on my head. As the moment calls for, I was sitting on the floor with my knees tucked up and my head bent over. I waited for her to kick one leg over me and then sit on my head, so I could take her feet and hold them braced on my knees in order for her to stand up at a precarious angle. She did the first part, but when she sat on my head, she burst out laughing. I felt her whole body shaking on top of my head, and I broke up. There we were, Darci sitting on my head and the two of us in hysterics. If you're not in a serious mood, that pas de deux is nearly impossible to dance. The rehearsal was over from that moment on.

Darci and I have a great rapport. I often feel that I knew her in a former life. We can just look each other in the eye and start laughing. She once told me I look like and remind her of one of her five brothers. So for her, it seemed like she was doing this very erotic pas de deux with her brother. That was *not* the feeling we were after! Darci and I spent a lot of time in the rehearsal room. In fact, by NYCB rehearsal standards, it could be considered overindulgent. When we talked, it seemed that she was almost reading my mind. Other than Elaine Kudo, I have never met another dancer who feels about things the way I feel about them. And, as with Elaine, I also found myself physically attracted to her.

The 1986 Spring Season was to open on a Tuesday, and the night before we had the second annual event called "Dance with the Dancers." I went by myself. I saw Darci there and we started talking. It was a western theme, and I remember Darci dressed in an outfit that was somewhere between Madonna and Cyndi Lauper. We started dancing and she really let her hair down. She cast aside her ballerina image. It was wonderful because in such a sheltered, closed-off world, it's often hard to let yourself go, especially when you're working. Like most artists and their art, dancers only want to dance. Darci's independent spirit is another quality that attracted me to her.

My first performance with the NYCB was in *Prodigal Son* with Darci. I felt comfortable, in familiar territory so to speak, and so excited I didn't really need to warm up. I had never been so anxious about any performance. Actually, it wasn't so much nerves as excitement. I felt like a racehorse waiting at the gate. I knew what I had to do. I had been away from dance, and now I was back. I was ready to prove myself again. Only this time not as a young kid.

Elaine Kudo had gone to Israel and brought back little stones in three little tin boxes for me. I felt funny about feeling the urge to give away something that had been given to me, but I did it anyway. I gave Darci one of those boxes from Israel, as something appropriate to the biblical story we were about to perform. I think she was truly moved, almost as if she had never received a "merde" before. I wanted to do something for her, knowing she was extremely nervous and having problems about getting back on stage after being out with injuries.

Before the curtain went up, I thought about many things. Would the tempos be quicker than I was used to? I thought I'd dedicate the performance to Mr. Balanchine by doing what he'd want. But what was *that*? What *would* he want? There's no controlling what goes through your mind in those moments before a performance. Thoughts fly in so many directions and land in some very unexpected places. They jump from what you had for breakfast to something you were told to do in rehearsal four weeks ago, to whether you should pursue a potential relationship, to wondering why you're doing all this in the first place. I think a performer's brain goes into a performance mode that is unlike any other thought process. It's more like a dream state.

The curtain went up, the ballet began, I made my entrance and the tempo was—*slow!* I took all the excitement I was feeling and turned it into anger for that first solo. I turned better than I had ever turned before and jumped higher. I felt that everybody in the company was in the wings watching.

Darci made her entrance as the Siren and was tentative at first. Everything was small and cautious. She didn't really dance her fullest. She seemed to be making the character very small. We started the pas de deux. To give her confidence, I held her tighter, pushed harder against her breasts and tried to make her forget her nerves and hesitation. Slowly it started to happen. I felt this was one time that instead of the Siren seducing the Prodigal, it was the other way around. At the least, I felt I was urging her to do something she was not ready to do at that moment. It was a different approach, but as valid as any other.

We finished the ballet. I was pleased, but I don't think Darci was. She knew that she could do better. We did three more performances and improved slowly with each one. It wasn't until the fall '86 season that Darci's performance improved to an enormous extent. She began to rely on her own instincts.

This reinforced my belief that a dancer can't cast him or herself in another dancer's mold. As much as you idolize or respect someone, you have to know what you like or adore in another dancer and, acknowledging that you will never *be* that other dancer, recognize who *you* are and what *you* have to give.

I've heard that one of the things that made Suzanne Farrell such a great dancer was that Balanchine never told her *how* to dance anything, he just let her dance it the way she would dance it. Suzanne understood that. She never really had to look at anybody. When she went on the stage, she was Suzanne Farrell. It's not that she was more important than the choreographer, but when she danced she was *as* important. That's what makes a great star. Balanchine appreciated that she did not need to copy anyone.

It's well known that over the years many dancers felt they had to copy Suzanne, but Balanchine never told them to. If he said, "Do like Suzanne does," he meant "Suzanne is doing what she does, now *you* do what *you* do." He made dancers look at other dancers to teach them how it looks to dance in your own way. He never wanted dancers to copy.

With Damian Woetzel (l) and Peter Boal (r) in Jerome Robbins' *Quiet City* (1986) (Photo by Paul Kolnik)

With Lauren Hauser in Robbins' *Interplay* (1986). (Photo by Paul Kolnik)

With Darci Kistler in Robbins' *Piccolo Balletto* (1986).
(Photo by Paul Kolnik)

With Heather Watts in Peter
Martins's *Concerto for Two Solo
Pianos* (1986)
(Photo by Paul Kolnik)

With Maria Calegari
in Jerome Robbins'
The Goldberg Variations (1987).
(Photo by Paul Kolnik)

As the "Pearly King" with Stephanie Saland, my "Pearly Queen," in George Balanchine's *Union Jack* (1986). (Photo by Paul Kolnik)

As the "Hoofer" (with Suzanne Farrell) in Balanchine's classic *Slaughter on Tenth Avenue,* (1986). (Photo by Paul Kolnik)

With Stephanie Saland in Robbins' *Opus 19: The Dreamer* (1987). (Photo by Paul Kolnik)

Photo by (Paul Kolnik)

Exploring narcissistic love with
Darci Kistler in Robbins'
Afternoon of a Faun (1987).
(Photo by Paul Kolnik)

The climactic "stolen kiss" in *Faun*, with Darci Kistler. (Photo by Paul Kolnik)

With Kyra Nichols in Jerome Robbins' salute to
Fred Astaire, *I'm Old Fashioned*, (1987).
(Photo by Paul Kolnik)

With Patricia McBride in Peter Martins' *Valse Triste*
(1987). (Photo by Paul Kolnik)

With Heather Watts in Balanchine's *La Source*
(1987). (Photo by Paul Kolnik)

With Kyra Nichols in *Other Dances* (1987). (Photo by Paul Kolnik)

In Robbins'
Dances at a Gathering (1986).
(Photo by Paul Kolnik)

With Patricia McBride in "Voices of Spring" section of Balanchine's *Vienna Waltzes* (1987). (Photo by Paul Kolnik)

With Darci Kistler in Jerry Robbins' *In G Major* (1987). (Photo by Paul Kolnik)

Caroline Cavallo and David
Hedrick with
vocalist Karen Mason
(center), in my ballet
Yesterdays for the School of
American Ballet Choreo-
graphic Workshop (July, 1987).
(Photo by Paul Kolnik)

Chapter 18

IT'S 1986. When I first walked into class with the New York City Ballet, there was Violette Verdy, this French bird, flying around the room, smiling and chatting before starting class. I had to smile because she's so adorable. I looked around in class and thought, Of course there are no dancers like there used to be in "the good old days," but look at what we *do* have.

I can't believe the abundance of talent that's in that company. To be in a room with ballerinas like Suzanne Farrell, Patricia McBride, Kyra Nichols, Heather Watts, Maria Calegari and Darci Kistler, you realize how incomparable they are. You can't compare them to dancers of an earlier generation, because today's approach to dancing is so different.

Any art form is a sign of its times. When we say there will never be another Gable or Garbo or Harlow, we're right, because they were products of a specific time and sensibility. Today's "stars" reflect our times, for better or worse. The great thing about film stars is that their performances are documented forever.

Dance is the only art form whose essence you cannot sit down and study totally recaptured. You can only read what critics or viewers said happened. Even Nureyev's dancing is not well documented. And for good reason. Dancing is a completely *human* art form. The human body is its essence. Man is becoming physically stronger and larger, and technique is developing so quickly that what Rudolf did in the sixties to astound audiences can be done by boys in the corps de ballet today. Also, documentation of dance can be dangerous. Two hundred years from now, people will look at our films and videos and wonder why we thought it was so wonderful. They won't know, because they weren't here. They didn't experience the feeling and sensibility of the times that contributed, along with the electrifying elements of personality, to the aura of someone like Nureyev. Film and video have no depth. The physicality is intangible. Of course that's not to say Rudolf wasn't a great dancer. He was a genius, the greatest dancer of his generation.

I've learned that one has to discover dance for oneself. You have to walk into a theater and be free of preconceptions and prejudice, have an open mind, see it as if for the first time. I never saw Violette Verdy, Diana Adams or Nora Kaye dance, but I've seen Darci Kistler . . .

Ballet must be the most poignant of the arts, because once it's gone, it's gone. There are recordings, there are films, books, paintings, but once dancers stop performing, they *stop*. There will soon be people coming to the ballet who never saw Peter Martins dance, who never witnessed his partnership with Suzanne Farrell. But for those who did see them, it's very hard to let go of that indelible impression.

We all know that was then and this is now, but it takes a great deal of objectivity and conscious effort to put aside your feelings and not be prejudiced by something that touched you so much. It's a lot like love. It's hard to cast aside feelings for those whose memory still touches you and open your heart to let others in. In film you can hold onto the images created by Bette Davis and Meryl Streep at the same time. Celluloid is their medium. But dance is experienced through physical spontaneity onstage, the immediacy of what the

250

senses respond to twenty-five yards away across the orchestra pit and footlights. It's much closer than anything on television can ever get. Besides, unless it's a live telecast, a dancer being filmed or taped knows that he or she can stop for whatever reason, if need be. The magic element of spontaneity is lost. In the theatre, there's the need to survive, to make it through without any stops to the end, that the audience senses from the dancer. Of course, there are films and videos of Margot and Rudolf and Peter and Suzanne and Sibley and Dowell and Patty and Eddie, but those films rarely capture what captured your heart. That's the poignancy of dance.

Partners are different on and off stage.

Probably the most challenging partner for me personally, in the sense of being hard to figure out *how* to partner, is Darci. But the experience of dancing with her onstage has been a most enjoyable partnership. She's not a *difficult* partner, but she has difficulty explaining what she feels and needs from a partner.

In one rehearsal, Darci turned around when a step didn't quite work well enough, and she said, "You know, I need something . . ."

I said, "Darci, I need a slightly better description than 'something.'"

Of course she laughed. But it is difficult for a ballerina to explain to a partner what must be done, since men have the advantage. We know what they do, but they have no experience in doing exactly what we do. So it's hard for them to explain what we need to do to help them.

Patricia McBride is one of the world's prima ballerinas. Like Natasha Makarova and Suzanne Farrell, Pat McBride walks onstage and the audience bursts into applause. And like Makarova and Farrell, she's one of the few ballerinas that I think separates the women from the girls.

Patty has danced with nearly all of the great male dancers

251

of our time, from Edward Villella, Helgi Tomasson and Ib Andersen, to Peter, Rudi and Misha. Yet, I have never felt an ounce of nerves in dancing with her. Her love of dance is still so strong, it's hard to believe she's been dancing with the New York City Ballet since 1959, the year I was born. There's a strange kind of thrill knowing this when I dance with Pat. She treats me with such respect, I feel like her contemporary. When you dance with her and she smiles that radiant smile, you just want to dance your heart out. The stage comes alive with her presence.

Sometimes when we're rehearsing, things may not be going quite right. She tries to help by saying, "Support me here! Go faster! Get me over my leg. *STOP!*" Then, when it seems nothing will work, Pat will say, "Oh, Robby, just let it *happen!*" Onstage there's never a calculated moment. Every performance is completely different. That's the McBride secret. Pat just lets it "happen."

Letting it happen is part of what NYCB offers me, and others, as a dancer. Even in the corps de ballet, a dancer has great individual freedom in the New York City Ballet. Once you learn a ballet you are free to rehearse it yourself without a ballet-master. You learn the steps, then go into the rehearsal room on your own. This is a major difference between NYCB and ABT. Dancers are basically being prepared to get onstage and dance on their own. In performance you can't have someone standing in front of you to say, "No. Stop. That's not quite right." Of course, you learn the ballets from the ballet-masters, then Peter Martins or Jerry Robbins comes into rehearsals and makes comments. When they are at work on other ballets, you have progressive rehearsals on your own. When you get onstage, you're free. You have to be yourself.

At Ballet Theatre, ballet masters and mistresses rehearse you all along the way. They teach the ballets, call for and supervise all rehearsals right up to final stage and dress rehearsals, and then, all of a sudden, you're out there onstage

252

by yourself. There's going to be a noticeable hesitation at first. I don't know whether Balanchine initiated his approach consciously or not, but it was an extremely important thing. Dancers can be so well directed and so well coached that it has a good effect, but a dancer can also be so overdirected that there's little left that's spontaneous or real about the performance. There's a certain danger in never being given enough independence and flexibility. You can't teach a bird to fly in a cage, then suddenly open the door and expect it to soar into the sky.

Part IV

THE LOSS...
AND LIFE

Chapter 19

N EW York City can be a brutal place to live in. Many leave the city to escape it; others who have to live there—like me—find other ways to escape. Let me share one with you.

In the fall of 1981, Kenneth and I rented a new apartment on West Seventy-first Street, a large one-bedroom with a big kitchen. But we didn't want to give up the studio on Broadway, in hopes that one day we would be able to use it as an office or as rehearsal space for singing.

At the time, my friend Lola Herman was looking for an apartment. I asked her if she would like to sublet 2020 Broadway for a while, and she did. It was at that point that the Empire of Assertania came into being, and became a cohesive element in the lives of myself and many of my friends.

Louis Branco created Assertania. Louis, a designer and art dealer, is part of the New York City art scene. He loves nightlife and is always interested in creative people. We met him through Peter Fonseca. When he and Lola Herman met at Peter's loft, they became very good friends.

Louis had come up with the nickname Lola Jean Merkel for Lola, and imagined she was married to a ne'er-do-well named Ed Merkel. One night around Christmas time, Louis and Lola were visiting friends, playing Scrabble, drinking champagne and wearing togas. Lola stood on a stool to have her hem fixed, and Louis stood back and said, "That's it! Merkelvania! You're the Empress of Merkelvania!" At that moment, Merkelvania was born.

So, Lola took a cab back to 2020 Broadway, feeling very pleased with herself that someone had just designated her an Empress.

Merkelvania came first, and Lola immediately declared that in Merkelvania there would be no litter. People did not litter, and people used their intelligence to take care of one another. From the kingdom of Merkelvania came the Empire of Assertania, a name also thought up by Louis. A name meaning, to 'assertain', to assert. In other words, in this Empire, you 'assertain', or understand, and then you assert yourself.

Assertania had divided into four Kingdoms by spontaneous combustion! Tirania, ruled by the von Outhausens; Transylvania, ruled by the von Cassins; Merkelvania, ruled by the von Merkels; and, Outer Cosmosia/Inner Cosmosia, ruled by the von Stratas.

At one point, the Empress inherited the Empire from her grandfather. Her father is the Archduke Marmaduke Farduke von Merkel. The Empress has been going it alone for some time now.

The Empire went on peacefully. People were human, just as they are everywhere, until Assertanians suddenly found themselves in the "Bubble." Being that the Empire is a state of mind, it can be anywhere and everywhere at the same time. Assertania came to the "Bubble" during the Disco Era.

What, you may ask, is the "Bubble"? It's New York. It's Cincinnati. It's the U.S. of A. It's wherever we are at any given point that is *not* Assertania.

Assertanians are bringing certain principals of Assertania to the Bubble. Word spread like wildfire. The group has become very large. There's a family tree with the names of hundreds of people . . . Assertania is forever growing . . . No one had to be invited, they came banging on the door. It was bigger than Girl Scout Cookies—and the Empress is *crazy* about Girl Scout Cookies.

When people come to Assertania, they find their own niche. Assertanians choose their own names and tune into the particular Kingdom they're from. Von Outhausens are people driven with one perfect objective in life. Von Cassins are people attracted to the "glitterata" and show business, but not just artistically; for the von Cassins, Life itself is one continuing opportunity to entertain people. Von Stratas are those people who you know in Life, but you really don't know how you came to know them. (Got that?) Von Merkels are an amalgamation of all the kingdoms. Some keep the names they bring in from the Bubble, others relate to their calling in Life, some are dubbed by the Empress herself. Here are a few:

Empress Renata von Merkel II, the People's Choice Empress.

Louis is Prince Egon von Merkel, the Empress's nephew.

Gary is Prince Fabu (short for "Fabulous") von Cassin, Vice-Admiral and Prime Minister.

Our friend Alberto Corzo became Porto von Outhausen, the Empress's consort. (Porto is always off somewhere on a ship looking through portholes.)

Kenneth is Sir Wryly of Walter von Cassin, Governor General of Inner Dementia.

Charles is Prince Paste von Outhausen.

Andy Wentink was named Count Escribito von Merkel, Court Scribe, by the Empress.

I am Prince Apollo von Outhausen. (I immediately gravitated to the von Outhausens.)

Coming to Assertania is like reading a book, you fold yourself into its reality. Assertania doesn't substitute for our reality, it's another *kind* of reality.

In Assertania, Life imitates Art.

Assertania is based on love. People use their intelligence to deal with situations, and if that idea can be spread throughout the Bubble, Peace will reign.

That's not to say that in Assertania nothing can go wrong. Things do. There are so many small uncharted regions of Assertania that anything can happen. One night, for example, Horatia von Cassin was an hour and a half late for a dinner engagement with the Empress and Prince Fabu. Horatia finally called, full of apologies, to explain that her carriage had broken down in Egoslavia. It happens. Any one of us might someday be stranded in Inner—or Outer—Oblivia!

I would never become involved with something that is guru-oriented. I love the Empire. It's wonderful. It's all about believing in make-believe. It brings another dimension to our reality. You can walk into Assertania and become another you, an alter ego, relate with others and laugh again. From the beginning I liked Assertania's sense of wit and lightheartedness. The wit in Assertania comes from the idea of working out whatever we have to deal with in life on a lighthearted level. Assertanians strive to be serious and laugh at the same time. It's something that allows people to live their lives completely on their own terms. As the Empress says, "It's us and God."

Assertania is about what's happening to us in the eighties. It's about developing a family within your circle of friends. It's a kingdom where away from your natural family, wherever you are, you can create a familylike existence, a unity, a tribe. There's something very positive about it. You become a part of something you can depend on.

At first Assertanians met at small social gatherings. But in October 1985 it was decided that a large party would be held, where *The Obligata Proclamata* would be read, formalizing the ideas behind the Empire. Until that time we lived day by day taking our friendships for granted.

The *Obligata Proclamata de l'Amour* (The Proclamation of the Obligation to Love), penned by Fabu von Cassin (Gary Lisz), is a formal statement of the communal state of mind and bond of friendship based on love and concern for the world we live in that is Assertania. A standard of behavior and inspiration for all Assertanians. The Empress immediately knew these ideas to be true.

The October party was held around Halloween at Peter Fonseca's loft. People came in outrageous costumes and it was a great success. A stage was set up in one corner of the loft, and extemporaneous performances took place. Gary read the *Obligata Proclamata* to an enthralled gathering. John Kelly, one of New York's most outstanding performance artists, did an impromptu scene from *Carmen*. John later received the Obie Award for his performance at Dance Theater Workshop in *Pass the Blutwurst, Bitte,* a piece inspired by Egon Schiele that the New York *Times* rated one of the ten best performances of the year. The whole evening was very "downtown."

Although the atmosphere was lighthearted, the large group felt a strong sense of community in light of what was happening around us; the knowledge that some of our friends were very sick and might die soon.

With the success of the October party, the Assertanians planned a Spring Bacchanale party, to be held on March 15, 1986, between Albert Einstein's birthday and St. Patrick's Day. It was called "Green=mc[squared]."

Gary and I wanted to do a theatre piece, something for everyone. As we started our work, we realized we were basically developing a theatre group reminiscent of the commedia dell'arte, a kind of improvisational street theatre where everyone has his task in bringing together the theatre piece, and then all going onstage to perform at the end. We wanted to create original theatre art without answering to anyone but ourselves.

We decided to do an original ballet based on the Greek myth of Persephone, something Gary had always wanted to do.

The story of Persephone, is, of course, the mythological expla-nation of the coming of spring. One night, Gary and I were lis-tening to Stravinsky's "The Rite of Spring," and considered using it as the music for *Persephone.* Gary had written a sce-nario, and as he started reading it along with the music every-thing fell into place with such extraordinary coincidence, we could almost believe Stravinsky had written it for us. It was so unbelievable, it knocked us to the floor. When choreograph-ing to an already written piece of music, it normally takes a great deal of work to fit your conception to the music. This was just the opposite. The music pushed the scenario along.

The ballet was to be performed in Peter Fonseca's loft. Peter had been on tour and came back to New York to choreograph a ballet for his mother's school in Bethesda, Maryland. But when he got back he was too sick to work.

Peter had been having one physical setback after another for some time. He had a terrible problem with an extra bone in his ankle that would give him tendonitis, and he had an operation. He was recovering from the operation and was out of work for a very long time, some three or four months. He was on crutches and he would go home to Washington and come back frequently, since he wasn't working.

When he started back to work, Peter found he never really regained his stamina. I don't know the details of the operation—other than he had both ankles done—but he just never really got back into shape after that. He was always too tired. He went out on the road with ABT and couldn't do *Theme and Variations* and the pas de trois in *Swan Lake.* He just couldn't get through them. His excuse to himself was that he just wasn't in shape yet. But it was already three months after his return to dancing. So, it became obvious to many of us that there was something more wrong than just that. He started going to doctors and they weren't sure what was wrong. They thought it was an iron deficiency, because he did have iron-poor blood.

By March 1986 Peter was very ill, but he wanted the party and performance to take place in his loft just the same.

It took me about a week to choreograph *Persephone.* Although I had originally intended to have no major commitments that spring, I had by that time accepted Jerry Robbins' invitation to join the New York City Ballet and was just starting rehearsals. It left little time to rehearse for my ballet. But preparations continued.

Gary was busy decorating the backdrop one day early that week when the phone rang. It was our friend Dr. Barry Gingell.

"Gary, I've been telling Andy [Warhol] about the party and theatre piece, and he wants to know if he can come with his cameras to tape and photograph it."

"Oh, I don't see why not," Gary answered casually after catching his breath. "That's fine." He hung up, and screamed out loud. "Oh, God! Andy Warhol is taping *Persephone!* This is Pop Art Heaven! This is turning into real ART!"

A few days later Gary went to our writer friend Couri Hay's apartment to help out on the two hundred invitations we were sending. When Gary got there, Couri introduced him to this very conservative, unpretentious woman who Couri had invited to the party.

She said, "How do you do?" and they had a nice talk.

Later, when Gary was telling us about the afternoon at Couri's and got around to mentioning that he'd met this nice lady named Sydney Biddle Barrows, we gasped and one of our friends shouted, "Gary, don't you know who she *is*?" He had no idea. "Gary, Sydney Biddle Barrows is the 'Mayflower Madam'!" It blew him, and us, away. Andy Warhol and the Mayflower Madam coming to Assertania on the same night. We couldn't believe it. The Empire was spreading!

Peter was home in New York during the dress rehearsal for the Assertanian party *Persephone.* Our friend Jamie Cohen, who is exceedingly well built with huge muscles, was portraying Hades. Gary was Dionysus, the narrator. Except for a little loincloth, Gary didn't have on the elaborate costume or full-body makeup he would have in performance. Peter was lying on a couch, watching. The curtains parted, and Gary stood there half-naked. As Gary moved "downstage" to speak, Peter said, "Excuse me, shouldn't Jamie Cohen be playing this role?" Sick or not, Peter's wit was in fine shape.

Peter felt too tired and ill to see the performance in his own loft. He spent that evening with our friend Robert Lord.

March 15 arrived. It was very gala. There was a competition for the official Assertanian flag. An elaborate Assertanian family tree made by Louis hung on the wall. As always there were lots of wonderful costumes, many togas. In fact, when *People* magazine took a poll later that year about togas in honor of the Statue of Liberty Centennial, Sydney Biddle Barrows said, "I haven't worn a toga since my last spring bacchanale!" The Empress wore a casual white organdy and blue-dotted Holly's Harp dress and, of course, a tiara!

It seemed that the two hundred invited guests brought even more friends. There was an overwhelming feeling of unity. *Persephone* was an enormous success and was video-taped for posterity by Andy Warhol. We were all amazed to see how in such a short time the seeds of our creative ideas had been brought to such flower in the nurturing climate of Assertania.

The only time I've gotten truly depressed, even hysterical, was when I was in Paris and heard about Peter Fonseca. After a wild two-week tourist trip through Italy in August 1986, Gary and I were looking forward to an exciting week in Paris, living it up at the Plaza-Athenée. We were to meet Charles there. The day of our arrival, Charles called. He told us the doctors had gotten back the results from Peter's tests. He had a terminal illness.

I broke down on the spot and left the room. I couldn't control myself. Eventually, I pulled myself together and walked back into the other room to be with Gary. It was Paris at sunset. We stopped sobbing, walked out on the balcony and said, "Oh God, look at the Eiffel Tower. Look how beautiful Paris is." And then cried again. It was a strange, cruel irony that we could be reminded of the glory and incredible beauty life has to offer and at the same time know that our dear friend was going to die. We tried to have a good time, but we couldn't forget. We'd go from high spirits to low in seconds, telling jokes one minute and bursting into tears the next.

We went to dinner at St. Germain and everything reminded me of Peter. The entire conversation was magnified by reminders of him. Food didn't taste the same. It wasn't Paris anymore. It was just a table. Thousands of miles away on another continent, I felt helpless to do anything. We forced ourselves to enjoy the rest of the stay.

As we walked through Jeu de Paumes, Gary reminded me that the Impressionist masterpieces we were looking at inspired the costumes he had designed for *Voyage des Enfants*, Peter's last ballet. A very Impressionistic piece, it was choreographed for his mother that premiered at a gala performance. No matter where we looked, our thoughts were of Peter.

The last three days, we were ready to come home, ready to deal with the next, inevitable phase of our lives. When you move away from someone you don't see for a long time, it's almost like death. I felt dead for Peter. I wanted to get back and be there for him in whatever way he needed me.

Until Peter's illness, disease and death had been on the periphery of our lives. Even though we knew Peter was sick, we pretended for a long time that it was an iron deficiency, like the doctors first said, and that he would be fine. Sometimes he slept for eighteen hours a day. One night when we were out to dinner, Peter fell asleep at the table. Waking him, we offered to take him home, but he insisted that he was fine and only needed some coffee. But on our return from Paris, we had to face the reality.

Back in New York, Charles and I immediately made plans to visit Peter, who was at home with his mother in Washington, D.C. He was bedridden and under the care of a hematologist. The doctors said there was really no drug that could improve his condition. They gave him two months. Knowing that, I just wanted to be next to him and hold his hand.

Arriving at the house, I was suddenly afraid I wouldn't say or do the right thing. He was sleeping when I walked into the room. He was sleeping a great deal. The first and last thing I remember from those visits were his eyes. They were so completely wide open. He looked at everything with the intensity of someone who was seeing the world for the first time. He had the television on at all times. Charles had bought a large baroque pearl while on tour in Japan with ABT and brought it to show Peter. Taking the pearl from Charles, Peter examined it closely, touching it, turning it round and round, feeling its cool smoothness.

We spoke to him, but he didn't respond. In the time that we had been away, he had lost his ability to speak. He must have known what we were saying, because when we said funny things, he'd laugh. Every now and then he did manage to say "Bye-bye."

His illness had developed very slowly until some tests seemed to traumatize him. He became nauseous and too weak to stand up. His decline was very rapid after that.

It was raining that December morning in New York in 1986. I've always hated flying in bad weather, but private fears were not my major concern. I made it to the airport just in time to catch the 8:30 A.M. flight to Washington, D.C. I was supposed to meet Florence Pettan, but she wasn't on the plane when I boarded. I assumed she had overslept or was delayed in getting to the airport. I opened an issue of *Time* to calm myself when a stewardess brought me a message from Florence. She got to the airport early and took the 7:30 A.M. flight to D.C.

It was raining in Washington, too. Florence was waiting there at the airport when I arrived. She was relieved to see me, having thought I might have not gotten the message and decided to wait. We hailed a cab in the rain and proceeded to our destination. We had exactly thirty minutes to get there and the cab driver told us it was at least forty-five to fifty minutes away. Florence told him to get there as quickly as possible. We exchanged few words in the cab. There was little to say.

We were late in arriving at the church, but not as late as we had feared. A young priest, probably in his mid-thirties, stood at the door. We hurried by him into the church and took the first available seats. Looking around the church, I was surprised to see it was only half-full. I couldn't tell who was there, since I only saw the backs of people's heads. What I did know was that regardless of who was there, we had all come for the same reason—our love for Peter Fonseca.

Peter's mother and brothers sat close to the coffin, holding on to those last moments with Peter's body. I couldn't help feeling their deep sorrow. Twenty-eight years is not a long time, even for a life richly lived. The service wasn't long. A few songs were sung and at one point, the priest asked those of us in attendance to turn to the people close by and exchange our feeling of love for one another. It was a touching moment that I will cherish for a long, long time. I couldn't stop thinking of a time when we were discussing getting old and dying, and Peter told me that when his time came, he wanted there to be a joyous celebration of singing and dancing.

I felt guilty that now that the time had come, I couldn't do what he had wanted. Funerals are a peculiar thing. Each church and religion has its own way of handling them, yet none seems truly adequate. At times during the service, I felt that we were getting the standard, impersonal version of a eulogy, with Peter's name inserted where there had been a blank before.

After the service, people filed down the aisle and it struck me for the first time that this was *real*. I would never again see Peter dance or hear his voice. We were all there for the same reason, to cling on to Peter, not wanting to let him go. As people gathered in the church lobby, I was overcome by a strange, uncomfortable feeling. A social setting was not the proper place to be right now. I wanted to be alone.

It's unbearably sad when a close friend dies. You sense the absence of someone you knew and spoke to every day. The feeling is not just an emotion. It's physical. Your whole physical being feels collapsed and weighted down.

Suddenly, I lost control and started to cry. The reality was too strong for my emotions to bear. I already missed Peter and there was nothing I could do to bring him back. He was truly gone. I tried to justify his dying so young. "Only the good die young" didn't come close. Death is harder on those that are left behind.

Stepping outside the church, I saw that the rain had turned to a downpour. The heavens seemed to be crying for Peter. Everywhere I looked, people in black with black umbrellas were moving silently through the rain to their cars.

For those who couldn't attend Peter's funeral in Washington, Charles and I organized a memorial celebration in New York. I danced *Symphonie Concertante,* Second Movement, with Susan Jaffe and Cheryl Yeager; Cynthia Gregory and Peter's brother Paul spoke, and Gregory Osborne read a poem he had written.

Then Charles got up to speak. "The last time I was with Peter," Charles told the audience, "I went to visit him at his loft. I walked in and saw Peter sitting on the floor painting a malachite-like pattern of green and black stripes throughout this large area, with extraordinary detail. I have this thing about paste jewelry and was wearing several conspicuous pieces. Looking up at me, he gave my outfit the once over and said, 'Charles, how can someone in your position go around dressed like that?' I looked down at Peter and the beautiful floor he was creating and said, 'Well, does a dancer *deserve* to live in such palatial surroundings?'"

"Charles," Peter retorted, "if you can look like Catherine the Great, *I* can live in her palace!"

Everyone laughed, knowing how well it demonstrated Peter's wit and dedication to beautifying the world around him. Painting that floor was the last thing Peter did. I got to paint one little circle in the floor and signed my name in it, and Peter signed his name. When the floor was finished, we put in place a platform up to another level of the loft, covering my name. I didn't mind. My circle took ten minutes to do. It took Peter three weeks to paint the entire floor.

It was a perfect example of what made Peter who he was. He enjoyed details like that. He enjoyed setting a table for a dinner for eight, with placemats just so, candles and silverware perfectly matched, with everything color coordinated and the music setting the right mood and tone. The courses were served at the right time. Everyone was made to feel they were dining at Lutece. It gave Peter great joy to go to such lengths to serve at the dinner table. We all have special ways of making people happy.

Others at the service spoke of Peter's beautiful dancing, but Charles didn't choose to show that side of Peter. He chose something that really characterized *Peter* as a person. Everyone knew Peter's dancing. They knew how he would be the first to take new dancers under his wing, instructing them in the workings of the company, even to small details like filling out overtime sheets. He was always helping other people. It was his nature to make sure that the new people felt like a part of the whole thing. He didn't want anyone to feel ignored. He would teach dancers new ballets. He would stay after work with them. Everyone knew those things about Peter. It was an unusual trait in such an egocentric business to be so concerned and helpful to others, and one I'll never forget.

Peter was the first of our close friends to die. Now we deal with it almost on a weekly basis. Now that it's a part of our lives, I can finally say that I have come to accept Peter's death. The one thing I can't do is cross his name out in my address book. I don't want to say he's gone with a stroke of the pen. You cross someone's name out of your address book when your relationship is finished. His not being here was not decided upon by him or us. My relationship with Peter isn't finished. He's just not physically here, and when I die I intend to continue where we left off and proceed to the next level.

Two years before Peter's death, his father died. Peter took it very hard. It changed his life. He started going to church every Sunday. He was always a good Catholic, but like so many others when they come to New York, hadn't gone to church all the time. There were other changes. He became very strict about his regimen. His friends started to change. He started to dress more conservatively.

Gary always felt that Peter's life was so much about living, he approached life like one big festival. Many people, myself included, have a hard time accepting their own mortality. With the loss of his father, Peter had to face death for the first time and to realize the relatively short time we all have here. The changes in his lifestyle seemed to be his reconciliation with that awareness.

Peter's death made me face my own mortality. I know that someday I will die, and if I were to find out it was coming sooner than I expected, I would continue to do what I'm doing now, because I'm doing what I want.

Growing up, I heard about older friends who had lost loved

ones in Vietnam, and I could never appreciate what that must have felt like. Death is something I always connected with old people. Young people aren't supposed to have to deal with it. Then something like war or AIDS comes along. I've started to think. AIDS is like a war, only in war there's always someone to blame. No one is exempt from the threat of this plague, yet society still considers it a gay disease. A punishment for sinners. Many people, straight and gay, don't have the AIDS test because to many it carries the stigma of being gay-related. Dying has become an ugly thing, an embarrassment. I never thought of death as an embarrassment. It's horrible that society can impose humiliation onto other human beings who are dying.

Chapter 20

I 'M grateful that I have found something in my life that I love, that I'm good at and that is paying off, like ballet. Is this kind of public success and acknowledgment anything greater than a family sitting in their living room in Middle America watching "Live from Lincoln Center" on television, wishing they have what I have? I have my bad days with what I do, and I have my good days and, ultimately, I'm really not that much different from that family watching TV.

Perhaps it's my concern with being rewarded, and the fear of going unrewarded that has pushed me into this situation of being successful. I was determined to be rewarded.

I know my own success wasn't based on talent alone. I always believe that people who really achieve success in the ballet world do so with something else other than physical talent. Because if that were true, the people who could do more pirouettes, or jump higher, or do better fouettés, would always be at the top. But, it's not. You're in the hands of other people who are in control. Those people can make or break you. But then there are those dancers who have such a will, a desire to be there, to always go on, to fill in for other people— that success comes from sheer perseverance. Other people *will* themselves to success. They just want it so much that they sacrifice whatever is needed to get it.

It's like children who want to be the "best child." They will do whatever they have to do to be the best child. I spent my whole childhood wanting to please my parents. I wanted to please my teachers. I wanted to please Marsha Woody. I wanted to be better than anyone else at what I did. I wanted to be a good boy, the best. I know I was lucky that I found something I was in love with. I was in love with the idea of dancing and performing on stage. But my whole life has been centered around pleasing people. I often feel the need to say "the right thing" rather than saying what I truly feel. Whenever I'm faced with a situation where I have to make a decision, be it political, artistic or emotional, it's typical of me to have a conflict. I'm afraid of not being rewarded by "the family" or "the company." But more times than not, I somehow manage to get out of these situations what I really want.

One of the best things I ever did was to leave American Ballet Theatre. I started to ask myself, Why are you so unhappy? Why are you feeling this? Why? And there were some hard things that I had to deal with. I was unhappy with a great situation, and people couldn't understand why. How could I explain that I was unhappy with a career, people who loved me, people who wanted to see me dance all the time? If you're unhappy you've got to try to understand why. And so I finally said, "I want to give it all up. I want to bite the dirt."

I wasn't feeling "rewarded." I was always trying to be rewarded. I wanted to be rewarded for all of that. But I wasn't. I was being a good little student, a good little boy . . . And it was getting me nowhere. I needed rewards, true, but the reward I needed was freedom.

Misha was this extremely talented boy from Russia, who grew up and had everything he wanted in Russia *except* his freedom to do whatever *he* wanted to do, and he figured it out. He got everything he wanted to do when he got to America; all he had to do was say it. I'm still searching but now it's a little easier.

274

I'll never forget four years ago a psychic said I had fierce energy, that my career was going to go, go, go. He saw me going to London to become a director. He also said I was a writer. He said, "I know you're a dancer and that you're dancing, but what you really are in life is a writer."

"What are you talking about?" I said. "I don't even write letters."

But he saw me writing—if I didn't let this "dancing stuff" get in the way.

At the time, everything was happening for me at ABT and I couldn't understand what he was trying to say. Perhaps today, even after writing a book, I'm still not a writer, but I do know that I haven't let dancing—or anything else—get in the way of leading my own life.

Index

Index